ALTERED!
ART PROJECTS

A Tweety Jill Publication
by Jill Haglund

ALTERED! Art Projects
First Edition 2008
Copyright by TweetyJill Publications, Inc.
All rights reserved. No part of this book may be reproduced or
transmitted in any manner whatsoever without the written permission
of the publisher except for projects not for resale.

Published and created by:
TweetyJill Publications, Inc.
5824 Bee Ridge Road, PMB 412
Sarasota, FL 34233

For information about wholesale,
please contact Customer Service at
www.tweetyjill.com or 1-800-595-5497.
Ask for free flyer detailing all books.

Printed in China
ISBN 978-1-891898-14-3

Book Design: Laurie Doherty & Michelle Glines
Book Layout: Jill Haglund
Managing Editor: Lisa Codianne Fowler
Photography: Herb Booth of Herb Booth Studios, Inc.
Photo Stylist: Jill Haglund

ALTERED!
What does it really mean?

altered (ôl'tərd) adj. changed in form or character without becoming something else; v. to make or become different

The term "altered art" conjures up different visions and ideas for every individual. Artists seem to be especially adept at finding their own unique meaning for anything they decide to label "altered". Some artists may say, "that's not altered" or another may say "that is definitely altered" or still another artist might think, "that's sort of altered" about the same piece of artwork.

We decided to create a book titled "ALTERED! Art Projects" that would appeal to all types of artists, from scrapbookers to those who do mixed media and assemblage artwork.

Impossible you say?

If we simply look at "altered" as something that has changed from the original concept, every work on every page falls under that category. A simple canvas or a photo has a complete metamorphism just like a caterpillar to a butterfly... tear, distress, texture, collage, surround with mementos, add embellishments and ephemera; enclose in a frame or shadow box and voila… ALTERED! It is no longer a simple canvas or the same photo. The artists bring new life by the changes they add. And with the saturation of inspiration and creativity, the piece becomes not only something changed but something more meaningful. That is part of the artists' gift to us. We thank them profusely for that, for without thinking beyond what is initially seen, there would be no altered art form.

We can't wait for you to feast your eyes on the breathtaking collection of all the fabulous altered art featured in this book: birdhouses, shadow boxes, window panes, wooden hearts, bowls, framed collages and scrapbook pages, boxes, bottles, suitcases and much more. Some of my favorite pieces are the western-themed shadow boxes by Carlene Federer and Deb Trotter and the "Red Robin Ranch Birdhouse" with a western touch by KC Willis.

We know you'll find joy in creating these fun and inspirational projects, that, with your personal touch, will become your own works of altered art. ...western or not!

Creatively Yours,
Jill Haglund, Founder
TweetyJill Publications

Table of Contents

Chapter 1 - Altered Boxes

Chapter 2 - Altered Framed Collages

Chapter 3 - Altered Shadow Boxes

Chapter 4 - Altered Birdhouses

Chapter 5 - More Altered Stuff

Grandma's Sewing Box
Lou McCulloch

MATERIALS

Rubber Stamps: Remember and Lost Memories Slab by Postmodern Design

Dye Inkpads: Memories Black by Stewart Superior; Tim Holtz Vintage Photo Distress Ink by Ranger

Papers: Matte Photo Paper by Epson; Transparency Film (0.10mm)

Adhesives: Glue Stick; Multipurpose Adhesive Spray by 3M; JudiKins Diamond Glaze

Other: Tall Paper Mache Box with Lid; Images of Old Quilt Squares; Image of Relative (or any person you would like to showcase); Various Shaped Buttons (about 10); Old Lace; Ribbon; Buckles or Hanging Beads

Tools: Fine Sandpaper; Scissors

I wanted to make a copy of my great-grandmother's photograph and use it in my artwork. Since it was a tintype, I knew it would be best to print in black and white, so I decided to try printing it on a transparency. I found myself staring at the image that resulted, for it seemed to have a three-dimensional quality. This portrait of Alice was taken on her wedding day when she was fifteen years old. She seems to be bravely looking forward to her life on an isolated farmstead. The theme of the box was "quilts", because Alice became a wonderful seamstress, passing down through the generations her quilt creations. I am lucky enough to have some of her treasures.

Perhaps you can also showcase a treasured relative and copy their creations on to an assemblage of yours. What a wonderful gift it would make!

INSTRUCTIONS

1. Lightly sand edges of paper mache box and lid to allow distressing to adhere to the edges more easily.

2. Set printer to "transparency" under paper settings. Print your favorite image onto a sheet of transparency film. Be sure to print on the side that feels rough to the touch, otherwise your image will not adhere well and will smear. Cut around image and set aside.

3. Arrange copies of quilt squares around the sides and top of the lid until you are happy with the results. Cut the papers to fit and attach with glue stick. Ink edges of box with Distress Ink. Stamp "remember" in black onto a ribbon.

4. Center transparency on the front over a quilt design. Lightly spray top of quilt design and back of transparency with adhesive. Wait ten seconds, then apply transparency. Add the word ribbon over the transparency with Diamond Glaze.

5. Add buttons around the edge of the lid, gluing in place with Diamond Glaze.

6. Thread a scrap of lace through a vintage buckle and attach with glaze. Add an old celluloid chain with a crocheted ball on the end to drape down the side of the box.

This vintage photo of the little cowgirl needed to be honored. The expression on her face suggests that she is dreaming. Imagining. My interpretation of that expression is that she is fantasizing that one day she too will be a grown up cowgirl. The layer upon layer of images and words represent the many possibilities that await her.

Cowgirl Congress Cigar Box Purse

Deb Trotter

INSTRUCTIONS

1. Sand and clean cigar box.
2. Randomly tear small pieces from an old western-themed book. Cover the entire cigar box inside and out with gel medium and torn pieces. Be careful that gel does not get on hinges. Let dry or speed up drying with a heat gun. Repeat with a second layer of torn papers. Seal all sides, inside and out, with two thin coats of varnish. Dry.

continued...

MATERIALS

Rubber Stamps: Western Central Kansas Cowboy, Rodeo, Sidesaddle, Back at the Ranch, Home Sweet Home and Ridin', Ropin' and Wranglin' by Viva Las Vegastamps; Outlaw by Beeswax; Horseshoe by Stampscapes; Bullet Hole by A Fistful of Stamps; Cowboys by Acey Deucy; Desert Post by Toybox; Running Horse by KK Originals

Dye Inkpads: Memories by Stewart Superior

Paints: Gessos and Grounds by Golden; Burnt Umber Light, Burnt Sienna, Quinacridone Gold, Phthalo Blue (Red Shade), Payne's Gray and Cadmium Red Medium Hue Fluid Acrylics by Golden; Antique White Creamcoat and Matte Interior Varnish by Delta; Clear and Amber Bulls Eye Shellac by Zinsser

Stickers/Rub-Ons: Horse Stickers by Karen Foster Design; Cowboy Elements Collection by Creative Imaginations; Cowboy Borders Collection by Marah Johnson; Nostalgiques Paper Buttons, Key, Tape Measure and Letters by EK Success

Adhesives: E-6000 by Eclectic Products; Matte Gel Medium by Golden; Krazy Glue

Other: Set 13 Pendleton Cowgirl Mini Collage by The Queen's Dresser Drawers; Star Paper Fasteners by Creative Imaginations; Workable Fixatif by Krylon; Ribbon Stacks by Prima Marketing; Vintage Photos; Old Book Pages; Raffle Ticket; Curly Q Wire; "Smokin' Cowboy" Stamp; Small Rhinestones; Stars; Cigar Band; Metal Heart; Small Gold Hinges; Indian Wooden Nickel; Metal Chain Belt; Gun Keychain; Western Charms

Tools: Scissors; Xacto Knife; Heat Gun; Bone Folder; Electric Sander; Electric Drill; Clamps

The most valuable advice I can offer when creating a piece like this is to experiment with layers. Glue, gesso and paint are your best friends. Continue to add more and more papers, images and words. Paint some of them so that they barely show through and paint others only slightly. The blend of gesso and paint is the key. The great thing about this layered technique is that if you don't like what you've done, simply paint over it and start again. The other secret to the look of this piece is the amber shellac. It produces that final "glow" of intrigue and antiquity.

Cowgirl Congress
Cigar Box Purse
continued

3. Paint random portions of the box with *thin* coats of gesso; dry. Next, add thinned gesso mixed with Antique White paint; dry. Paint sides and edges of box with Phthalo/Payne's Gray mixture and Cadmium Red/Burnt Sienna mixture as desired. Dry.

4. Using dye ink, stamp western designs randomly all over box, inside and out. Spray with Krylon Fixatif. Dry for ten minutes. Lightly paint over parts of the stamped designs with a mixture of gesso and Antique White paint. Dry. Spray again with fixatif.

5. While box is drying, cut out various sizes of photographs and set aside.

6. Begin to collage vintage cowgirl/cowboy images to box using gel medium. Do the same with interesting text from old western books.

7. Now is the time to experiment with layering. Place smaller or larger images over those that are already adhered. Paint over some and leave some as they are.

8. Add the western stickers or cut-outs randomly in a pleasing composition to complement the existing images. Lightly paint some of these with the gesso/paint mixture, and other random areas with Quinacridone Gold.

9. Stamp more words or images on the top of the painted areas. Continue to add layers of paper buttons, words, tape measure, concho trim on front and more small images until you are pleased with the result.

10. Paint the edges of the inside of the box with Burnt Sienna and Burnt Umber Light to achieve a peeling paint effect.

11. Shade around some of the words and images with Burnt Sienna or Burnt Umber Light.

12. Sand all edges inside and out with an electric sander for a worn paint appearance (you may just use sandpaper if you like, but the electric sander really speeds up the process).

13. When you are satisfied with the layered look, apply two thin coats of Delta varnish. Let dry.

14. Following the directions on the container, coat the entire box with two thin layers of the Zinsser Amber Shellac. Let dry overnight and then apply one coat of Zinsser shellac. Let dry for six hours.

15. Decide on placement for the hinges on top of the purse near the opening. Slip the end of link chain inside each hinge. Glue hinges to box with E-6000. Secure with clamps. Wait at least two hours. Use small drill bit on the wood beneath hinge holes and hammer nails in place.

16. Cover nail holes on hinges with star brads. Add tile letters that spell out "COWGIRL CONGRESS".

17. Embellish with ribbon, gun keychain and western charms.

Mica Nesting Box
Lisa Cook

MATERIALS

Rubber Stamps: Small Alphabet Set by Ma Vinci's Reliquary

Papers: Ledger Paper; Vintage Scrap

Adhesives: Glue Stick; Elmer's Clear Caulk

Other: Mica by USArtQuest or Volcano Arts; Fabric; ¼" Foam Board; ⅛" Eyelets; No. 19 DK Annealed Wire; JudiKins Diamond Glaze or Polyurethane Varnish; Pictures; Ribbon; Silk Flowers; Coffee-Dyed Label

Tools: Eyelet Setter; Hole Punch; Pliers; Craft Knife and Mat; Ruler; Soldering Iron; Lead-Free Solder; Flux; ¼" Copper Tape and Patina Chemicals by Delphi

INSTRUCTIONS

1. Using craft knife, cut foam board to desired size for a box.
2. Adhere desired papers, words and pictures to foam board with glue stick.
3. Apply a protective finish (glaze or varnish) to foam board pieces and let dry thoroughly.
4. Cut mica to fit the box.
5. Adhere mica to foam board.
6. Punch holes and attach eyelets to lid and top of the back for hinges. Adhere rose spray picture to lid.
7. Use copper tape to attach the box sides and bottom together; solder.
8. Run copper tape around the lid and solder.
9. Finish the soldered areas with desired patina chemicals.
10. Cut wire and bend with pliers to form two hinges for the box.
11. Front: Adhere ribbon; position coffe-dyed #2 label over blue ribbbon snippet. Sides: Adhere ribbon snippets and silk flowers onto side panels.

See page 19 for Mica Shell Box

I wanted to create special boxes that would entice the holder to look inside. A lightweight mixture of transparent mica and foam-core board provide the base for these boxes as opposed to glass. Individual inspiration for each box came from the lovely vintage images I found in old damaged children's readers as well as Victorian "shell art" often featured on boxes and mirrors. I drew parallels of nests and home upon images of calm and protection for the largest box drawing.

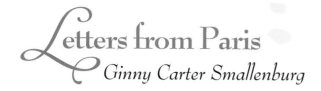

Letters from Paris
Ginny Carter Smallenburg

MATERIALS

Rubber Stamps: Scratches, Dutch Birth Certificate and New York Central by Stampers Anonymous; Par Avion Set by Small Studio Productions

Dye Inkpads: StazOn Jet Black, Blazing Red and Brown by Tsukineko

Papers: Rusty Pickle; K&Company; Rossi ATC Background Paper by Small Studio Productions

Paints: Daisy Cream Patio Paint by DecoArt; Butterscotch Adirondack Acrylic Paint Dabber by Ranger

Stickers/Rub-Ons: Stickers by Small Studio Productions

Adhesives: Incredi-Tape and Crystal Clear Tape by Coffee Break Design; The Ultimate! Glue by Crafter's Pick

Other: Wooden Box; Tag; Ribbons; Trims; Two Acrylic ATC (Artist Trading Card) Bases; Vintage Pen Nibs, Clock Charm; Vintage Clock Face; Faux Lens; Postcards and Gold Scrap by Small Studio Productions (or local craft store)

Tools: Foam Brush; Scissors

I love anything French and have quite a collection of French-themed ephemera: postcards, old letters from Europe and new French ribbons to use on my projects. The classic and timeless vintage look will never go out of style because it reminds us of a time gone by that we perceive as more gentle and kind and less hectic.

INSTRUCTIONS

1. Roughly paint entire wooden box with Daisy Cream paint; age with Butterscotch Dabber or foam brush.

continued...

OUTSIDE:

2. Cut pattened papers, distress edges with brown ink and layer on lid. Stamp and collage ATC background paper and adhere with double-sided tape to back of acrylic ATC base. Cut out female figure from sticker sheet and add to front of base. Next, adhere base with Incredi-Tape to front of box. Add ribbon banner, pen nibs and clock charm as seen on page 15.

3. INSIDE: Adhere and layer torn piece of wrapping paper, vintage clock face, postal sticker, lady sticker and ribbon to inside of lid. Add acrylic ATC base over female image. Finish with faux lens, small postal sticker and ribbon tie.

continued...

4. Line inside of box with patterned paper. Add suede eyelet tape to outside bottom half of box with double-sided tape.

5. Make bundle of letters using postcards and copies of vintage letters. Tie with French ribbon. Embellish tag with stamped images, stickers and gold scrap frame; add to box. Feast your eyes on an altered vintage creation.

SEA SHELL

MATERIALS

Papers: Vintage Scrap

Paints: Acrylics by Golden

Adhesives: Glue Stick; Elmer's Clear Caulk

Other: Mica by USArtQuest or Volcano Arts; ¼" Foam Board; ⅛" Eyelets; No. 19 DK Annealed Wire; JudiKins Diamond Glaze or Polyurethane Varnish; Pictures and Words from Vintage Children's Readers; Seashells

Tools: Eyelet Setter; Hole Punch; Pliers; Craft Knife and Mat; Ruler; Soldering Iron, Lead-Free Solder, Flux, ¼" Copper Tape and Patina Chemicals by Delphi

Mica Seashell Box
Lisa Cook

INSTRUCTIONS

1. Using a craft knife, cut foam board to desired size for box top and bottom.
2. Adhere desired papers, words and pictures to foam board with glue stick.
3. Apply a protective finish (glaze or varnish) to foam board pieces and let dry thoroughly.
4. Collage and paint larger shell as desired. Coat with protective finish and dry.
5. Cut mica to fit the four sides of the box.
6. Punch holes and attach eyelets to lid and top of the back for hinges.
7. Use copper tape to attach the box sides and bottom together; solder.
8. Run copper tape around the lid and solder.
9. Finish the soldered areas with desired patina chemicals.
10. Cut wire and bend with pliers to form two hinges for the box.
11. Adhere desired shells to lid with caulk.

The sea box map fragment and the girl in the sand remind me of days spent at the beach when I was young.

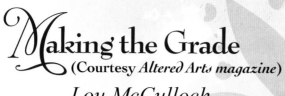

Making the Grade
(Courtesy *Altered Arts magazine*)
Lou McCulloch

MATERIALS

Rubber Stamps: Large Alphabet Letters by PSX (Personal Stamp Exchange); Word Stamps by Postmodern Design

Pigment Inkpads: VersaFine Onyx Black by Tsukineko

Dye Inkpads: Tim Holtz Walnut Stain Distress Ink by Ranger

Papers: Paper Reflections Script Alphabet by Creativity Inc.

Other: Small Cigar Box; Pinewood Blocks (the depth and size of cigar box); Vintage Images of Children; Alphabet Paper and Multiplication Table; Vintage Cloth Ribbon; Cardboard (for template); Small Pencil; Small Piece of Wire

Tools: Saw; Sandpaper; Dremel or Drill with Small Drill Bit

(Note: Pre-made boxes and blocks are available at www.theweathereddoor.com)

INSTRUCTIONS

1. Lightly sand edges of box and rub edges with walnut inkpad. Glue school-related ephemera and alphabet paper to inside lid and back of box.

2. Measure inside of box, making a template for the blocks. Transfer measurements to the wood. Sand edges of cut blocks.

3. Using the same template, divide vintage image into block sections. Stamp words onto image. Cut into pieces and glue to each block. An additional back image can also be attached to the blocks, if you wish. I also stamped large letters on the side of each block, spelling simple words such as, "cat", "play", etc.

4. Stamp words onto ribbon. Attach pencil with ribbon by placing two tiny holes in the lid and wrapping wire around pencil and through the holes.

$\mathcal{M}$y inspiration for this piece was the small cigar box and the worn green pencil I found at an antique store. I bought a bag of well-used pencils for $1.00 and the clerk asked, "What would you want those for?" I told her, "I just need pencils," otherwise she surely would have not understood my reason for buying them!

I had wanted to make some blocks to put photos on, but the unfinished blocks I had on hand did not fit in the box. I measured the sides and depth of the box and gave the measurements to my husband to custom cut twelve blocks with his saw. I printed out the photos in sepia, added text and rubber-stamped simple, common words on the sides of the blocks.

The text "Making the Grade" and "Try Again" seemed to fit with the two different photos of the children (I divided the class!). I have always loved school-related items, and found a copy of an old multiplication table to put on the reverse of the box. A scrap of alphabet paper and vintage cloth ribbon completed my school box.

aged RETRIEVED FROM CRASH

SEC. 562 P. L. & R.
U. S. POSTAGE
PAID
PERMIT 985

by Salt Water

by ship's catapult

In my collection of photographs I found a picture of dear little boy in a sailor outfit and decided to enhance it with anchor buttons. Then I thought of all the children that may have been lost at sea, or at least orphaned, so I stamped "retrieved from crash" and "by ship's catapult" to the arrangement. The highlight was the word "fish" on the top of the box.

I had recently returned from a trip to the Outer Banks in North Carolina, where I gathered some shells to add to my collection. I particularly look for small shells with tiny holes in them, which are easy to attach to surfaces with string. I had a small vintage box that had at one time contained codfish and was perfect for a sea theme.

A Boy at the Sea
Lou McCulloch

MATERIALS

Rubber Stamps: Word and Tamarind by Nick Bantock
Dye Inkpads: Van Dyke Brown by Nick Bantock
Papers: Matte Photo Paper; Cream Cardstock
Adhesives: JudiKins Diamond Glaze; Craft Glue
Other: Vintage Sailor Boy Images; Seashells; Small Wooden Box; Anchor Buttons; Sea Postage Stamps and Ephemera; Lacquer Spray

INSTRUCTIONS

1. Print vintage images on photo paper. Stamp cardstock and photo paper with rubber stamps as shown.
2. Randomly place images including postage stamps, inside and outside of the box, attaching to box with Diamond Glaze.
3. Position embellishments with craft glue as shown.
4. Lightly spray entire surface with lacquer.

I found a great little vintage Victor Hugo libretto of "Les Miserables" at what we call our local Recycling Barn --- a.k.a. the dump. We proud, local folk have what we call "The Gift Shop" within the belly of the barn. I cherish my Saturday morning trips to the shop… hubbie watching the kids at home and me all alone with a steamin' cuppa Joe and my favorite tunes as I leisurely drive over there. The shop is filled with junque -- not just junk, but the more beautiful spelling of the word, as this junque represents to me all kinds of artistic possibilities -- treasures and trinkets that will find their way into my art. Like in this piece, "Twinkle, Twinkle," created on the vintage book cover of the "Les Miserables" book I found, all dusty on the gift shop shelf. The tie-dyed look of the background already existed on the original book cover, so all I had to do was make the foreground scene. It is amazing how someone's discarded objects can be totally reinvented and given new meaning beyond their functional properties -- becoming art.

CHAPTER 2
Altered Framed Collages

Twinkle, Twinkle
Susan Tuttle

INSTRUCTIONS

1. Use 5" x 7" or 8" x 10" canvas for collage base. Paint as desired. This happens to be a book cover used "as is".

2. Alter boy image with Photoshop Elements and print out.

3. Paint boy's stockings with white acrylic and let dry. Accent with black marker. Add purple oil pastel as a border around edge. Cut image.

4. Adhere collage elements, including fabric and newspaper, with Mod Podge or gel medium.

5. Apply a light wash of gesso to the ground imagery. When dry, add faux stitches with black marker.

6. Outline house and heart with charcoal pencil. Outline canvas edge or book cover with purple water-soluble oil pastel.

7. Using the small bristle paintbrush, make celestial dots in the sky in a random fashion.

8. Prime photo frame with gesso and allow to dry. Paint with white acrylic and let dry.

9. Add metal strips to top and bottom of frame. Adhere ribbon to frame edge.

10. Insert collaged canvas into frame and

MATERIALS

Papers: Found Vintage Papers

Paints: White Acrylic; Gesso

Markers/Pens: Black Zig Fine Tip Marker by EK Success

Pastels/Chalks: Purple Water Soluble Oil Pastel by Crayola; Charcoal Pencil

Adhesives: Mod Podge by Plaid or Gel Medium by Golden

Other: Fabric Scraps; Adhesive-Backed Metal Strips by EK Success; Red Ribbon; Star Punches; Scan of Vintage Image of Boy; Photoshop Elements by Adobe; Photo Frame; Canvas or Book Cover

Tools: Scissors; Fine Bristle Paintbrush

The Vintage Man

Kristen Robinson

I have always been completely enthralled by vintage photos. Whenever I find them in an antique store or even at an estate sale I find myself contemplating the lives of those pictured in them; wondering who they belonged to, where they lived, who they loved and who loved them. Above all, I often wonder who could discard a photo so easily.

MATERIALS

Rubber Stamps: Vintage by Hampton Art

Dye Inkpads: Van Dyke Brown from Nick Bantock Collection by Ranger

Papers: Watercolor Paper (140 lb.)

Paints: Cream and Rust Acrylic Paints; Rust Crackle Finish; Olive and Copper Watercolors

Pastels/Chalks: Water Soluble Oil Pastels by Binney Smith

Colored Pencils: Prismacolor Sienna Brown by Sanford

Adhesives: Craft Glue

Other: 4" x 6" Unfinished Wood Frame; Copper Tape; Vintage Image of Man; Pencil

Tools: Paper Trimmer; Paintbrush: Bone Folder; Circle Template

INSTRUCTIONS

1. Paint frame with rust acrylic paint, set aside to dry.

2. Use a dry brush to paint watercolor paper (cut to fit the insert of your frame), with cream acrylic paint. Use very quick strokes to avoid any thick layering. Set aside to dry.

3. Apply crackle medium to frame per package directions. Apply a layer of cream acrylic paint over the medium and set aside to crackle.

4. Randomly shade edges of watercolor paper with olive watercolor or crayon. Repeat with the copper watercolor or water soluble oil pastel.

5. Dip a small detail paintbrush into water (or use your fingertip), dab onto a paper towel and lightly go over your colors making sure that you blended them in a few areas.

6. After the background has dried, adhere your vintage image. Use a bone folder to ensure it has completely adhered.

7. Place a piece of copper tape below the photo, using a bone folder to smooth and firmly adhere.

8. Use either a circle template or the bottom of a glass to draw a circle around the man's head in colored pencil. Go over the circle with copper watercolor or brown water soluble oil pastel and blend with small amount of water.

9. Add shading with the sienna colored pencil.

10. Stamp the word "vintage" above the photo.

11. Add a strip of copper tape to the top of your frame, again using the bone folder to smooth and adhere.

12. Place the completed piece in the frame and enjoy your creation.

The stoic pose and very serious expression of the man in this vintage image inspired me to place him in a not-so-perfect looking frame while adding a bit of copper tape to accentuate his photo. Perhaps he was a man of wealth, or simply a man who borrowed a friend's suit for a special photo. I will leave it up to you to decide. Who do you think this man is?

Instructions on page 28.

A World to be Born In

Kristen Robinson

MATERIALS

Rubber Stamps: Postage Stamp by Cavallini & Co.
Dye Inkpads: Memories Brown by Stewart Superior
Papers: Blue Diamond Paper by Creative Imaginations; Ledger Paper by K&Company
Paints: Black Acrylic
Colored Pencils: Prismacolor Sienna by Sanford
Adhesives: Craft Glue
Other: 7 Frame; Brown Checked Rick Rack Trim (adhesive-backed) from Wild Asparagus by My Mind's Eye; Gaffer's Tape by 7gypsies; Blue Ribbon; Copper Brad; Copy of Vintage Image; Favorite Quote; Black Letter Tiles
Tools: Scissors; Paper Trimmer; Paper Piercing Tool

INSTRUCTIONS

1. Paint frame black.
2. Cut diamond paper to fit the frame.
3. Tear a strip of journal paper and adhere to center of background.
4. Place a strip of Gaffer's tape about ¼" from the top of the background and cover the width.
5. Pierce a hole in the left side of rick rack. Place brad through blue ribbon and then through hole in rick rack. Dab glue under ribbon to secure.
6. Apply rick rack approximately ½" from the bottom. Press firmly to ensure adhesion.
7. Stamp the postage stamp image in brown ink onto the right-hand side of the background. Place image on background, making sure to smooth out any air bubbles.
8. Print or stamp your favorite quote, cut it into strips and adhere to the right of image. Highlight around the words with colored pencil.
9. Ink all the edges of the card with brown ink.
10. If you will be using this as a playing card, draw or stamp the appropriate suit and number onto your card in the location of your choice.
11. Once frame has completely dried, sand all the edges lightly to distress.
12. Adhere letter tiles to the bottom center of frame.
13. Frame your artwork and enjoy!

This year I began participating in an ongoing card project. It is a wonderful idea as each week there is a theme assigned with a particular playing card. The artist creates their card based on the interpretation of the theme, and the best part is we keep our own work - which is something as artists we rarely do. It is a most phenomenal project to be involved in and has become a bit like Christmas as one waits wondering what lovely works of art will be created next. The theme for this card was favorite quotes. As I love working with vintage images of children and this quote by Saint John Perse is one of the best I know, I thought it would be a perfect addition to my deck.

Wild, Precious Life

Jill Haglund

MATERIALS

Paints: Light Pink and Cream Acrylic; Quinacridone Gold Fluid Acrylic by Golden

Adhesives: Liquid Stitch by Prym Consumer USA

Other: Three-Dimensional Magnetic Frame by Melissa Frances; Thin Batting; Rose Patterned Fabric; Cheesecloth; Laundry Bleach; Instant Coffee; Petroleum Jelly; Vintage Buttons; White or Off-White Printable Fabric by Color Textiles; Photo; Quote

Tools: Sewing Machine; Foam Brush; Needle and Thread

Creative gift idea for any family member.
Simply choose a photograph of meaning to them.

INSTRUCTIONS

1. Cut a piece of rose patterned fabric and a piece of 5" x 5" cheesecloth to fit frame. Add a cup of laundry bleach to small load in washer or soak fabric in pail; squeeze moisture from fabric. Dry.

2. Make a coffee dye by simmering a quart of water and adding two to three tablespoons of instant coffee. Dip pre-washed, faded patterned rose fabric and the cheesecloth in the pan; be careful when handling warm and wet pieces. Allow to dry, preferably on a line outside. Press flat. Your fabric and cheesecloth are now ready to use.

3. Print out desired photo and quote with printer onto white or off-white printable fabric. Cut out. OPTION: Age fabric with brown spots using a light wash of Quinacridone Gold Fluid Acrylic (test a piece of fabric first). Apply to fabric with a lot of water and your finger.

4. Cut a piece of batting slightly smaller than photo and quote.

5. Arrange cheesecloth in a pleasing manner to show attractive elements of patterned rose fabric. Adhere cheesecloth with Liquid Stitch.

6. Layer batting piece to back of photo and both to fabric using same adhesive. Let dry 20 minutes.

7. Sew a straight stitch along edge of photo to secure it onto fabric and cheesecloth. Glue batting and quote onto photo and stitch.

8. Use a needle and thread and sew all vintage buttons in place by hand.

9. Paint frame with cream acrylic paint. Once dry, wipe with petroleum jelly here and there. Paint pink acrylic on frame near petroluem jelly areas. Allow to dry. Wipe off all petroleum jelly to show distressed look.

10. Encase all in frame. Close and display.

A Moment in Time
Deb Lewis

MATERIALS

Rubber Stamps: Vintage-Style Wording
Dye Inkpads: Brown
Papers: BasicGrey; Black Cardstock
Paints: Black Gesso
Stickers/Rub-Ons: Rub-On Text by Making Memories
Adhesives: Glue Stick
Other: 5" x 6" Shadow Box Frame; 5" x 7" Canvas Board; Paper Heart Embellishment; Press-On Rick Rick by me and my BIG ideas; Vintage Photo Transparency
Tools: Scissors; Bone Folder; Paintbrush; Heart Punch

INSTRUCTIONS

1. Paint a 5" x 6" shadow box frame black and set aside to dry.

2. Randomly stamp wording and phrases in brown ink onto a 5" x 7" piece of BasicGrey paper.

3. Adhere stamped paper to canvas board with glue stick. Smooth down paper with bone folder, eliminating any air bubbles that may have occurred during the gluing process.

4. Adhere vintage photo transparency to stamped paper background, again using glue stick and bone folder. Allow to dry completely.

5. Use bone folder to apply rub-on text, your chosen words or phrases, onto paper. Use a blank sheet of paper over the lettering to make certain it is firmly in place.

6. Place the press-on rick rack trim into position and as before, rub over with a blank piece of paper to secure.

7. Adhere paper embellishment such as a heart punched out of vintage text adhered onto black paper. Trim black paper close to heart shape. Dry. Attach to rick rack as shown.

8. Attach the finished canvas board to the inside of the painted shadow box frame. You now have a finished piece ready to hang!

As a child I spent endless hours sifting through dusty trunks in my grandmother's attic. I was always fascinated by the yellowing photographs of my ancestors, especially those of children. Many afternoons were spent creating fanciful stories to give these photographs a life of their own.

This particular piece was inspired by the photograph of the sweet young girl, who looked a bit lost and in need of her own "story" to recreate a little moment in time.

Les Fleurs
Deb Lewis

After spending an afternoon looking through my photos of Paris, I came across a picture I had taken of a gorgeous flower store we visited during our last trip to my favorite city. Immediately I found myself thinking of this vintage photo of the two sweet little girls with their flower basket who look so very Parisian.

MATERIALS

Rubber Stamps: Various Words and Phrases

Dye Inkpads: Brown

Paints: Black Acrylic

Papers: Decorative Tissue Paper

Adhesives: Glue Stick

Other: 5″ x 6″ Shadow Box Frame; 4″ x 4″ Canvas Board; Metal Heart-Shaped Brads; Rusted Metal Bookplate; Vintage Image

Tools: Scissors; Bone Folder; Paper Piercing Tool or Hand Drill with $^{1}/_{16}$″ Drill Bit

I created this piece to try to convey my deep love of Paris. I imagine these two darling children walking along the streets of the city with their lovely flowers, drawing patrons with their adorable sweetness and delightful bounty of French flowers…. "Les Fleurs".

INSTRUCTIONS

1. Paint shadow box frame black and set aside to dry.

2. Randomly stamp wording and phrases in brown ink onto a 4″ x 4″ piece of patterned tissue paper.

3. Adhere decorative tissue paper to canvas board. Smooth down the paper with a bone folder to eliminate any air bubbles.

4. Adhere vintage photo to tissue paper background and smooth with bone folder.

5. Insert a word or phrase into metal bookplate; insert a metal brad into the holes of the plate.

6. Use a paper piercing tool or a hand drill to create two holes for the brads to go through and attach bookplate to piece. Note: If the canvas board is too thick to penetrate, adhere bookplate with an aggressive adhesive and let dry completely.

7. Insert your piece into painted shadow box frame to complete.

This piece embodies all of my favorite things…from the image, to the colors, to the ribbon. When I am placing one of my collages in a frame, I find I often alter the frame prior to using it, making it part of the artwork rather than just a house for it. This little girl is one of the images I tend to use a lot when creating pieces that spotlight children. I adore the sweet look on her face and really felt I wanted to surround her with a bit of fun and whimsy. So, I rounded up some whimsical paper, the wonderful striped ribbon and a couple of my favorite stamps and went to work. When I look at the completed piece it makes me happy - which is exactly what I want the viewer to experience.

Best Times (top right)

Kristen Robinson

INSTRUCTIONS

1. With a dry brush, paint the frame Antique White, using short fast strokes with minimal paint. Allow to dry.

2. Use Mod Podge to adhere stamped ledger paper randomly around edge of frame. Set aside to dry.

3. Cut a piece of red polka dot paper to fit inside the frame.

4. Tear a strip of the book page and place at the bottom of polka dot paper as shown.

5. Adhere a thin strip of torn floral paper to the left-hand side of the polka dot paper.

6. Glue thin red striped ribbon to perimeter to create a border. Place one red button over the ribbon in each of the bottom corners.

7. Apply Antique White acrylic paint to foam stamp and stamp in the center upper portion of background (within the ribbon frame). Set aside and let dry.

8. Adhere butterfly wings to back of photo and adhere photo to center of collage, smoothing out edges to remove any bubbles.

9. Create a party hat from a scrap of paper and adhere to top of head in photo.

10. With a dry brush, randomly stipple Baltic Green and Antique White acrylic paint. Set aside and let dry.

11. Highlight areas around the photo with red and brown crayons, within stamped image as well as around the border.

12. Stamp the 1937 Postal Stamp toward the bottom-right corner of your collage.

13. Place three copper brads in top center of frame. Secure and lightly tap the tops with craft hammer.

14. Tie three small strips of ribbon to the bottom-right corner of frame.

15. Insert collage into frame to complete.

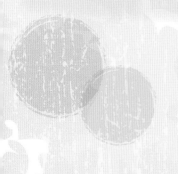

Balloon Baby Claire
Kristen Robinson

MATERIALS

Rubber Stamps: Oh So Pretty by Rubbermoon Stamp Company

Dye Inkpads: Tim Holz Brushed Corduroy Distressed Ink by Ranger

Papers: Ledger Paper by Making Memories; Heart Quotes by Marah Johnson; Lullaby Pink Check by Daisy D's Paper Co.; Green Embossed Paper; Book Page

Paints: Cream and Pink Acrylics; Pink and Brown Watercolors or Pink and Brown Water Soluble Oil Pastels by Binney & Smith

Adhesives: Craft Glue

Other: Thin White String; Thin Pink Ribbon; Vintage Image; 4" x 6" Unfinished Wooden Frame; Pencil; Book Page

Tools: Paper Trimmer; Paintbrush; Xacto Knife; Scissors

INSTRUCTIONS

1. Choose an image of a child.
2. Paint the wooden frame with cream paint and set aside to dry.
3. Cut ledger paper to desired size of background.
4. At top of ledger paper draw a pinking line. Fill in top area with either pink watercolor or water soluble oil pastel (colored pencils would work fine as well). Edge the scalloped area in brown again to add definition.
5. Adhere green embossed paper to bottom edge.
6. Glue fence covered with book page to background and add vintage image of child.
7. Cut out balloon shape, rub with inks and paints. Adhere to page. Add string with ribbon ties to piece and enclose in frame.
8. Stamp "oh, so pretty" on face of frame.

Road to Nirvana
Audrey Hernandez

I was inspired by this crow stamp, which I think is just the coolest. It made me want to create something kind of fun and funky... a little off the beaten path maybe. I also love fences, so I definitely saw this little guy sitting on one as if pondering where to go.

MATERIALS

Rubber Stamps: Oxford Impressions; Stampers Anonymous; River City Rubberworks; Postmodern Design; Hero Arts

Dye Inkpads: StazOn Jet Black and Timber Brown by Tsukineko

Papers: K&Company; NRN Designs; Scrap Ease; BasicGrey

Paints: Spotlight by Making Memories

Adhesives: Gel Medium by Golden; Black Artist's Tape

Other: Deep-Edged Chunky Canvas by Winsor & Newton

Tools: Scissors; Heart Punch

INSTRUCTIONS

1. Cover canvas with various papers using gel medium.
2. Cut up patterned paper to make fence posts and add to chunky canvas.
3. Use rubberstamps for script, titles, numbers, postage mark, crows and scratches on fence.
4. Add punched hearts to top with artist's tape.
5. Paint sides of canvas and, when dry, add fence posts to sides.

MATERIALS

Rubber Stamps: Angel with Wings by Toybox; Swirl by Making Memories

Dye Inkpads: StazOn Jet Black by Tsukineko

Papers: White Fibrous Paper

Paints: Pink, Sky, Espresso and Spotlight by Making Memories

Markers/Pens: Zig Photo Twins by EK Success

Stickers/Rub-Ons: Narratives by Karen Russell; Making Memories

Pastels/Chalks: Portfolio Series Water Soluble Oil Pastels by Binney & Smith

Adhesives: Gel Medium by Golden

Other: Deep-Edged Chunky Canvas by Winsor & Newton; Cherish Snap by Melissa Frances; Old Book Page; Hardware

Cherish
Audrey Hernandez

INSTRUCTIONS

1. Paint front of canvas in a variety of acrylics. Paint the sides brown.

2. Add old book page, white fibrous paper and rub-on words and letter.

3. On separate piece of paper, stamp angel in black ink and color in with pen; adhere to canvas.

4. Use acrylic paint to stamp swirl design on all sides of the chunky canvas.

5. Outline angel stamp with blue oil pastel and rub in.

6. Add hardware and "Cherish" snap.

I love this little angel boy rubber stamp and just had to use it for my canvas. I wanted the piece to have a warm, family feel to it and a sense of home, hence a little piece of funiture hardware.

Seek
Audrey Hernandez

MATERIALS

Rubber Stamps: Paperbag Studios; Making Memories

Dye Inkpads: StazOn Timber Brown and Jet Black by Tsukineko

Papers: Black Vellum

Paints: Pink, Brown and Spotlight Acrylic by Making Memories

Stickers/Rub-Ons: 7gypsies; Autumn Leaves

Adhesives: Gel Medium by Golden

Other: Deep-Edged Chunky Canvas by Winsor & Newton; Bird Image by Cavallini & Co.; Ephemera; Ticket Stub; Nest; Old Book Pages

Tools: Punch

Birds, nest, home, safety… these are all the things I wanted to capture on this canvas. And I made sure to bring everything to the center by making a faux filmstrip. I also added a warm glow by using browns and coppers.

INSTRUCTIONS

1. Adhere book pages randomly on front of chunky canvas.
2. Overstamp with various script and image rubber stamps.
3. Blend with white acrylic paint.
4. Adhere punched black vellum, add nest, hanging ticket stub and bird image.
5. Apply rub-on words and images.
6. Paint sides of canvas brown bringing paint in dry-brush style slightly to the front as shown.
7. When sides are dry, add rub-ons.

Cowgirl Starlight
Deb Trotter

INSTRUCTIONS

1. Make sure shadow box is free from dust and lint. Following the directions on the back of the bottle, apply two coats of Sophisticated Finishes Primer & Sealer to all major surfaces (outside and inside of shadow box, tin angel wing, metal Christmas star, metal fence and wood doll head knobs). Allow to dry overnight.

2. Use a sponge brush to apply one coat of Sophisticated Finishes Rich Gold Metallic Surfacer to all treated items. Dry with the aid of a fan (not a heat gun) for three hours.

3. Randomly apply one coat of Sophisticated Finishes Patina Green Antiquing Solution with a sponge brush to all treated surfaces. Let dry overnight.

4. Spray all treated items with fixatif.

5. Using a large, stiff bristle brush, randomly dry brush Golden Orange and red paints on all treated surfaces. Dab random areas with Ice Jade and Warm Violet inkpads (direct method). Let dry and spray with fixatif.

6. Glue all four knobs (which will act as the "feet" of the piece) to the bottom of shadow box.

7. Cut BasicGrey paper to fit inside back of shadow box and apply with Mod Podge. Cut four long strips (about ½" wide each) of coordinating BasicGrey paper and glue on top edge of shadow box.

8. Rub ink pads along top edge of box over paper.

9. Use E-6000 to glue large angel wing to top of shadow box, then glue metal star to center of wing. Secure both of these with clamps. Allow to dry for three to six hours.

10. Glue artificial flowers and moss to bottom of shadow box.

11. Cut out a piece of scrapbook paper in an accent color of your choice approximately 1" wider on all sides than the book cover. Accent edges of paper with Olive inkpad. Adhere book cover to paper with glue stick as shown.

12. Using E-6000, adhere a long wood block or some cork stoppers to the back of the book cover and paper backing to create dimensions; glue to the back of the shadow box.

13. Computer-generate vintage photos and text. Print out. Spray with fixatif.

14. Color cowgirl image with chalks as desired. Spray again with fixatif.

15. Cut out cowgirl image. Use glue stick to adhere to black cardstock. Cut out again. Apply pop dots to back of cowgirl and glue to right side of book cover. Cut cowboy image to fit frame and place in frame. Glue to book cover.

16. Rub fence with chalk and ink. Attach metal fence to bottom of shadow box.

17. Adhere stars to top corners. Spray with fixatif.

18. Embellish with dried flowers.

MATERIALS

Rubber Stamps: Slab Background Stamp (GE3-101-D) by Postmodern Design

Pigment Inkpads: Olive Archival Ink by Ranger; ColorBox Fluid Chalk Cat's Eye Ice Jade Inkpad and Warm Violet Fluid Chalk Inkpad by Clearsnap, Inc.

Dye Inkpads: Memories Cherry Red by Stewart Superior

Papers: BasicGrey Scrapbook Papers; Black Cardstock; Heavy Cardboard

Paints: Transparent Pyrrole Orange, Quinacridone Red and Cadmium Yellow Medium Hue Fluid Acrylics by Golden; Sophisticated Finishes Primer & Sealer, Rich Gold Metallic Surfacer and Patina Green Antiquing Solution by Triangle Crafts

Pastels/Chalks: Decorating Chalks by Craf-t Products

Adhesives: Matte Mod Podge by Plaid; E-6000 by Electric Products; Instant Krazy Glue (all-purpose with Skin Guard) by Elmer's; Glue Stick

Other: Wood Shadow box (made to order by local woodcrafter); Vintage Cowgirl and Cowboy Photos; Book Cover from Vintage Zane Grey Novel; Photo Charm; Metal Star Christmas Ornament; Pop Dots; Long Wood Craft Block and/or Cork Stoppers; Small Rhinestones; Matte Fixatif Spray by Krylon; Metal Fence Rustic Accents by Darice; Four Knobs 1-1/4" Size; Large Tin Angel Wing by Westwater Enterprises; Bag of Moss; Dried or Artificial Flowers and Leaves

Tools: Large Paintbrush with Stiff Bristles; Acrylic Paintbrushes (including a small "line" brush for detailing); Sponge Brush

ROUGH 'N' TOUGH

SOME LITTLE GIRLS STILL
DREAM OF BEING COWGIRLS
AND SOME COWGIRLS STILL
DREAM OF BEING
LITTLE GIRLS

This piece was created in memory of my childhood — watching TV westerns and dreaming of one day being a cowgirl. I was surrounded by our family dogs, my cousins, and simple, small playthings like marbles, tops and wood blocks. All of these things filled my world with wonder. It was my western heroes, however, who most sparked my imagination. To this day I'm a cowgirl at heart. The 50's was a great time to be a kid, and I am happy to say I was molded by those years.

Cowgirl Milestones
Deb Trotter

INSTRUCTIONS

1. Cover all four sides and front edges of shadow box with torn masking tape in a random fashion. Overlap tape and vary the tape size, totally covering the outside of shadow box.

2. Tear pieces from vintage western book and randomly glue to insides of shadow box with Mod Podge.

3. Paint outside of shadow box with combination of Butter Pecan and Titan Buff. Let dry. Randomly paint sides and edges with Golden acrylics.

4. Apply gesso inside the entire shadow box. Some areas should be thicker than others so that some of the words from the book pages show through. After gesso has dried, starting with the lighter colors and adding the darker ones, apply various Golden acrylics with a medium flat brush. Continue, letting paint dry and adding more until you are satisfied with the look.

5. Shade edges of shadow box with Memories Cherry Red inkpad.

6. Computer-generate vintage photos; print and cut out. Apply glue stick to back of photos and paste to black cardstock. Cut out with scissors or knife. Computer-generate words; cut out and set aside. To prevent inkjet ink from running, spray images and words with fixatif.

MATERIALS

Dye Inkpads: Memories Cherry Red by Stewart Superior; Tim Holz Vintage Photo and Mustard Seed Distress Inks by Ranger

Papers: Black Cardstock

Paints: Gesso Ground and Burnt Umber Light, Cadmium Red Medium Hue, Cadmium Yellow Medium Hue, Quinadricone Gold and Titan Buff Fluid Acrylics by Golden; FolkArt Butter Pecan Acrylic by Plaid

Stickers/Rub-Ons: "Rough n Tough" Sticker and Star Stickers by Karen Foster Design; "Pass" Rub-On by Making Memories, Vintage Photos

Adhesives: Matte Mod Podge by Plaid; E-6000 by Electric Products; Glue Stick

Other: Shadow Box (made to order from local woodcrafter); Painter's Masking Tape; Vintage Photos; Horse Christmas Ornament; Children's Wood Blocks; Marbles; Iron Star; Vintage Wood Flat Spinning Top; Resin Puppy Dogs; Computer-Generated Words; Vintage Photo; Bingo Piece; Flat Wood Block; Vintage Zane Grey Book Cover; Tin Stars Rustic Accents by Darice; Pop Dots; Matte Fixatif by Krylon

Tools: Small and Large Flat Acrylic Paintbrushes; Sponge Make-Up Tips; Scissors; Bone Folder; Xacto Knife; Plastic Clamps

7. Paint front of the flat wood spinning top with Golden's Burnt Umber light. When dry, adhere back of spinning top to a flat wood block (for dimension) with E-6000, then glue the block to the inside of the shadow box.

8. Glue pop dots to back of cowgirl image and adhere to front of spinning top with E-6000.

9. Apply "Rough n Tough" sticker to spinning top with Mod Podge.

10. Glue little girl photos to right side of shadow box, then glue metal stars to their dresses with E-6000.

11. Use E-6000 to attach iron star in left corner and horse ornament in bottom right of shadow box. Apply pressure with clamps until dry (at least six hours).

12. While star and horse are drying, glue down blocks, puppies, metal gun and marbles with E-6000.

13. After glue has set for 24 hours, lay shadow box down on its back. Use Mod Podge to affix words and paper stars above the horse. Apply "Pass" rub-on with bone folder.

14. Touch up shadow box by highlighting randomly with paint and inkpads (use make-up sponge tip applicators for the ink).

15. Spray completed shadow box with fixatif. Allow to dry for eight hours.

> **TIP** There are two keys to success with this type of piece. First, you must totally overcome any fear of painting. Play. Rework. Repaint. Enjoy the process. Secondly, scale and balance are everything. Try to keep the eye moving with the placement of objects in and around your shadow box.

Cowgirlz Just Wanna Have Fun *Carlene Federer*

MATERIALS

Papers: SEI Papers; Cardstock; Eat Your Carrots and Cornflower by Making Memories

Paints: Tan; Antique White

Stickers/Rub-Ons: Words By KI Memories; GinX Express-Ons Alphabet by Imagination Project

Adhesives: Mod Podge by Plaid; Spray Adhesive by 3M

Other: Shadow Box; Petroleum Jelly; Rhinestones; Sequins; Glitter; Vintage Cowgirl Images; Plastic Letters by Heidi Swapp

Tools: Paintbrush; Scissors

INSTRUCTIONS

1. Remove Velcro back of shadow box.
2. Paint box inside and out with tan paint, let dry completely. Apply a thin coat of petroleum jelly randomly over the box and paint over with antique white paint. Let dry again. Wipe off petroleum jelly.
3. Using Mod Podge, glue patterned paper to the outside front glass. Lightly wet the patterned paper and peel off in random areas, then add a complementary piece of striped paper behind it for depth.
4. Add rub-on words and flowers to the inside of glass.
5. Print cowgirl image onto cardstock, cut out.
6. Add sequins and rhinestones to cowgirl images, glue image to bottom of box.
7. Cut a border from another piece of patterned paper and glue to top and bottom of box. Apply title and sequins to border.
8. Lightly spray inside of box with 3M adhesive and add glitter to finish.

Here I go again with those vintage cowgirls! I SO love this image of these cowgirls! I just imagine what close friends they were, and how their life was an advebture together. All three of these cowgirls were on the rodeo circuit together, and I'm sure rodeo cowgirls were pretty rare, especially in their day, so they all stuck together and looked out for each other!

One of my favorite artsy techniques is to pair vintage images with bright, modern colors and accessories, which I did in a big way on this shadow box! Since I just know these girls are having fun, I wanted them to have bright papers and embellishments, so I gave them plenty of color, sequins and rhinestones!

$\mathcal{B}$uffalo Gals

Carlene Federer

MATERIALS

Inkpads: Embossing Pad

Embossing Powders: Ultra Thick Embossing Enamel

Papers: Vellum; Cardstock

Paints: Off-White; Dark Blue; Pale Yellow; Pink/Gold; Crackle Medium by DecoArt;

Adhesives: Mod Podge by Plaid; Pop Dots

Other: Shadow Box; Vintage Cowgirls and Moon Images; Glitter; Extra Glass; Stars; Rhinestones; Swirl Transparency

Tools: Embossing Gun; Paintbrush

INSTRUCTIONS

1. Remove Velcro back of shadow box.

2. Paint outside of box with off-white paint, paint inside of box with dark blue, let dry.

3. Following manufacturer's directions, apply crackle medium. Apply a coat of pale yellow paint to the outside of the box. Paint a coat of pink/gold to the inside.

4. Scan and print out or copy cowgirl and moon images on cardstock, cut out.

5. Emboss moon face with Ultra Thick Embossing Enamel, add glitter while embossing enamel is still wet.

6. Outline cowgirls and moon in pink/gold paint and glitter, add rhinestones to cowgirls.

7. Make a wash with the dark blue paint and lightly paint over the back peice of glass. Repeat this process with the pink/gold paint. Add glitter while paint is still wet. Let dry.

8. Glue stars and rhinestones to the back piece of glass.

9. Use pop dots to attach moon to the back piece of glass. Adhere the cowgirls in place in the same way.

10. Print song lyrics on vellum and glue to outside of frame.

11. Tear swirl transparency and glue to the inside of the frame; add the front piece of glass. Glue rhinestones to buffalo, spray with glitter and glue buffalo to the top of the box to finish.

TIP

You can jazz up this western shadow box by cutting and adhering a bright red bandana to trim out the sides of the frame.

$\mathcal{T}$his shadow box reflects my creative spirit and passion for the prairie life. Choose a theme or subject that inspires you and gather images and ephemera; computer-generate or stamp your favorite songs or quotes to add. Hop on the wagon train and have at it, partner!

BY THE LIGHT OF THE MOON...

47

*P*ensive Love

Kristen Robinson

MATERIALS

Dye Inkpads: Tim Holtz Antique Linen Distress Ink; Van Dyke Brown from the Nick Bantock Collection by Ranger

Papers: Newsprint and Patterned Paper by 7gypsies; Primitive Hearts by Rusty Pickle; Nursery Red Polka Dot Paper by Daisy D's; Scrap Brown Patterned Paper

Paints: Brown and Cream Acrylic

Colored Pencils: Prismacolor Black by Sanford

Pastels/Chalks: Black Charcoal Pencil

Adhesives: Mod Podge by Plaid

Other: Shadow Box (Original measures 5 ½" x 7 ½"); Bingo Piece, Vintage Photo; Cardboard Scrap; Matte Gel Medium by Golden

Tools: Foam Paintbrush; Paper Trimmer; Scissors, Xacto Knife; Bone Folder; Glue Gun (optional)

INSTRUCTIONS

1. Using a dry foam brush or a dry paintbrush, sparingly paint the outside of the shadow box with the brown acrylic paint, set aside and let dry. Apply cream acrylic paint using the same dry brush method.

2. Choose a vintage photo that covers at least three-fourths of the background. Create a hat to place on top of the head of the image in your photo; adhere. Apply a thin coat of gel medium to your image; set aside and let dry.

3. Mount a small piece of cardboard to the back of your image to help stabilize it; this will help later when adhering inside the box.

4. Measure background paper to be the same size as the back of the shadow box and adhere, making sure to smooth out any bubbles with a bone folder.

5. At the bottom of the background paper adhere a small strip of red polka dot paper and above that a strip of brown scrap paper.

6. Using a charcoal pencil and starting from the top center of the background, draw a triangle, but do not close it off with a bottom line. Smudge the edges a bit to add a bit of shading.

7. In the center of the point adhere a small bingo piece or other found object that fits your image.

8. Under the bingo piece add the word "Pensive" either stamped or printed onto a piece of scrap paper. Underline the word very lightly with either a charcoal pencil or a regular pencil.

9. Cut out one heart from the Primitive Hearts paper, being sure to leave the black background around it. (If you do not have this paper you can mount a red heart onto a black piece of cardstock to achieve the same effect.)

10. Place the heart as close to the front center edge of the shadow box as possible without touching the glass. Use either a hot glue gun or an extremely aggressive adhesive per packaging instructions.

11. Approximately ½" behind your heart mount your image using either a hot glue gun or adhesive.

12. Once you are sure the glue has dried, place the back on the shadow box and display it for all to see.

I found the woman in this photo to be very pensive. The expression on her face is full of thought, almost as if she is filled with sadness. As I do with any old photo I stumble across, I began to create a story in my mind, a story of perhaps what she was thinking when the camera caught her in her dreamy state. This piece seemed to have a mind of its own. As I was assembling it, each element presented itself to me as something that needed to be included. Like most of my artwork, however simple, I believe it is of full of message and hopefully of spirit.

TIP

Coat the wood of your shadow box with a sealer. This will help prevent fading as well as wear and tear.

MATERIALS

Rubber Stamps: Curiosities by Stampotique Originals

Paints: Light Blue Acrylic

Adhesives: Glue Stick; Aleene's Tacky Glue by Duncan Enterprises

Stickers/Rub-Ons: Rub-Ons by Making Memories and by Nostalgiques by EK Success

Other: Stars; Compass and Propeller by Fancifuls Inc.; Tags; Pewter Photo Corners by Making Memories; Posterboard; Map from Old Encyclopedia; Old Pictures of Amelia Earhart; Mica; Photoshop by Adobe (or other photo editing software)

Tools: Medium Foam Brush; Sandpaper

Eternal Flight Hero
Jill Haglund

TIP

Who is *your* hero? Gather photos, embellishments and ephemera and create your own Hero Shadow Box

INSTRUCTIONS

1. Add water to acrylic paint to make a wash and paint box as shown.

2. Add vintage map from encyclopedia or atlas page to background.

3. Cut out elements of Amelia from an encyclopedia. Scan photograph and use Photoshop to add more information if desired.

4. Mount images on heavy matt board to make them sturdy. Adhere to box.

5. Stamp CURIOSITIES onto scrap paper, tear and adhere to inside of box.

6. Add compass, "flight", silver stars, mica, propeller, tag and other embellishments.

I made this piece because I always admired Amelia Earhart for her courage. Being a pilot, I have always had a love of flying. I made this specific piece as a gift for my dear girlfriend, Karen Drews. Although we began our flying lessons at the same time, years ago, now she is a commercial pilot for a major airline. That was both of our dream at one time; I am so proud of her for following hers! I was meant to journey in a different direction.

School Daze
Lou McCulloch

MATERIALS

Paints: Pyrrole Red Fluid Acrylic by Golden

Adhesives: Glue Stick; Fabric Glue; Judikins Diamond Glaze; Double-Sided Tape

Other: Shallow Cigar Box; Old Tintype; Brass Heart Pin; Tacks; Picture Hanger; Old Buttons; Scraps of Homespun Wool; Tags; Stuffing for Heart; Lace; Old Quilt Squares; Belt Fastener; Vintage School Postcard; Pages from School Music Book

Tools: Sandpaper; Small Hammer; Tack Cloth and Nails

INSTRUCTIONS

1. Prepare cigar box lid by detaching from bottom and lightly sanding the surface and edges. Dust off with tack cloth.

2. Paint inside and outside of cigar box with Golden's Pyrrole Red, using a wide foam brush. Allow to dry overnight.

3. Attach a picture hanger to back center top with small nails.

4. Add quilt pieces to the inside of lid with fabric glue to form a background. Attach a brass heart pin or similar charm to the fabric.

5. Arrange ephemera, such as vintage music, old text or tags and attach to the fabric with double-sided tape. Use old tacks to secure the postcard and tintype. Adhere vintage buttons to box edges with Diamond Glaze, alternating colors and styles.

6. Cut out, stuff and finish seam on homespun heart. Add lace and belt loop with strip of old fabric.

7. My finishing touch was to add an "M" plastic hanger, which a friend had given to me, on the bottom of the tintype. This added something personal, as it is my initial and reminds me of my friend.

My inspiration was an old children's music book with the wonderful title of "Heart and Voice." One of the songs in the book was listed as, "How Shall the Young Secure their Hearts?" which fit in with my theme of "hearts" and "school." I have always collected old photographs, and the original postcard of the school children, circa 1910, fit perfectly. I wanted a photo of a child looking to the left, towards the center of the composition, and that's why I picked the tintype of the young girl. I needed another cloth item to accent the quilt pieces, so I added the homespun heart with lace and an old fabric tie through the belt loop.

I debated about the title for this tableau, but the children in the postcard appeared to be staring out into space with a dazed look on their faces. Thus the title, "School Daze."

James & Kim
by James' mother, Linda Moss, created
in a class instructed by Jill Haglund

MATERIALS

Papers: Deja Views and Making Memories

Pigment Inks: ColorBox Chestnut Roan by Clearsnap, Inc.

Adhesives: Glue Sticks; Glue Dots

Other: Wood Frame; Sepia-Toned Photos; Pewter Frame and Small Plaque with Brads from Making Memories; Three Small Tooth-Washers; Ribbon; Cheese Cloth; Buttons; Page from Vinatge Book; Silk Flowers

Tools: Paper Trimmer; Awl

TIP

Move and juxpose pieces until you are satisfied with the look of your scrapbook page before you begin to adhere the pieces. Simple types of collage elements such as these will look balanced and pleasing in an unlimited array of designs. Create your own custom layout.

INSTRUCTIONS

1. Cut all papers as shown.
2. Ink edges of pictures, papers and page from the vintage book.
3. Cut a piece of cheese cloth to layer under photo.
4. Once you decide on your design, begin to adhere layered pieces one at a time.
5. Beginning with bottom layer, glue all papers and inked paper strips. Add inked vintage page from book.
6. Position and adhere large and small matted/framed photos as shown.
7. Pierce paper with awl and add labeled plaque with brads.
8. Use glue dots to adhere all buttons and silk flowers.
9. Thread ribbon in tooth-washer and adhere to page corner; add other tooth washers.

Needless to say, this fabulous photo was the inspiration. All the pieces in the page were a part of a kit that Jill put together for a class at a scrapbook convention. This was my first attempt to adopt the use of unique embellishments such as tooth-washers and cheese cloth while scrapbooking.

Open the Gate

"Make a rhyme, and the gate will open for you."

Open the Gate

Debbie Overton

MATERIALS

Dye Inkpads: Archival Sepia and Adirondack Espresso by Ranger

Paints: Old Parchment Acrylic by Delta

Adhesives: E-6000 by Eclectic Products; Glue Stick; Matte and Gloss Gel Mediums by Golden

Other: Wooden Shadow Box; Gate by Oriental Trading Company; Pages from a Vintage Children's Elementary Reader; Copy of Vintage Photo; Antique Key; Vintage Buttons; Miniature Rose Vine; Butterflies; Moss Embellishments; Workable Fixatif by Krylon; Photoshop 7 by Adobe

Tools: Sandpaper; Sponges; Picture Hanger

INSTRUCTIONS

1. Lightly sand shadow box, wipe with damp cloth and let dry.

2. Scan vintage image into Photoshop, enlarge and manipulate as desired.

3. Cut out image and age with Sepia ink.

4. Spray print with fixatif. Allow to dry.

5. Paint shadow box with several coats of acrylic paint, allowing to dry between each.

6. Age box by lightly sanding edges.

7. Lightly sponge Espresso and Sepia inks randomly on box.

8. Seal box with two or three coats of gel medium. (Mix matte and gloss together for a satin finish.)

9. Adhere text and photo using glue stick or matte medium.

10. Work rose vine around gate.

11. Adhere gate, key, buttons, butterflies and moss with E-6000.

12. Attach picture hanger to back for hanging.

Seems everyone enjoys collecting vintage photographs now. Vintage photos of children caught in a moment of time are so priceless. The butterfly garden and gate are the perfect setting for this sweet infant photo.

*F*resh
Tia M. Bailey

MATERIALS

Paints: FolkArt Metallic Aquamarine and Metallic Copper by Plaid

Adhesives: Mod Podge by Plaid; JudiKins Diamond Glaze

Other: Small Chest of Drawers; Assorted Seed Pods; Pinecone; Feathers; Vintage Ephemera; Plexiglass; Ribbons

Tools: Plexiglass Cutter; Scissors

INSTRUCTIONS

1. Select a box as your base. The little chest of drawers trinket box was found in a thrift store.

2. Remove the drawers and shelves as desired. This piece has two levels because a shelf was left in place.

3. Paint the box with Aquamarine and then follow with Copper using whispy strokes.

4. Choose your embellishment pieces, such as feathers, a pinecone, seed pods and other items found in a large potpourri bag.

5. Play with the placement of your embellishments until you are satisfied with the way they look, leaving space for adhering your central image.

6. Cover the central image with Mod Podge to seal it into place.

7. Use Diamond Glaze to place embellishment pieces into the shadow box.

8. Optional: Add selected text from a dictionary or old book, or your own computer-generated words printed on paper.

9. Lay the box on plexiglass to measure the size to accurately cut to fit front of box.

10. Cut plexiglass down to size. Place it over the box to be sure it will fit properly.

11. Apply a fine line of Diamond Glaze to the edges of the box. Place plexiglass on box over the Diamond Glaze; hold firmly in place and allow to dry.

12. Accent sides and bottom with your favorite ribbons or trims.

This was created using items I found during my bargain hunt one rainy Saturday morning. I came home and opened up the window to listen to the sounds of the rain. As it continued to pour down outside, I poured my heart into working on this piece. The beautiful image of the woman along with the nature theme soothed me. This piece still gives me a feeling of peace and tranquility whenever I look at it.

fresh (fresh) 1. recently made, grown. 2. not spoiled 3. not tired, lively 4. new, recent

It was a happy moment when I opened my package of prints and saw these photos of my nieces — they were more than enough to inspire me to make this shadow box. Meghan is 14 years old, Ruthie is five and little Leigh is four. They have a special brother too — Johnny. But this shot was about sisters! These pictures are brimming with their personalities and I felt I needed to make something special for their mom and dad to display! The photo was taken right outside Grandma and Grandpa's house in Minnesota.

Sisters Forever
Jill Haglund

MATERIALS

Papers: K&Company
Paints: Off-White, Pink and Brown Acrylics
Stickers/Rub-Ons: Variety of Rub-Ons
Adhesives: Glue Stick, Spray Adhesive; Foam Tape
Other: Shadow Box; Chipboard Letters by Rusty Pickle; Pewter Frame by Making Memories; Rick Rack; Lace Trim; Silk Flowers; Rustic Wrought Iron Corner (from antique store)
Tools: Two Medium-Sized Foam Brushes; Screwdriver and Small Wood Screws; Sandpaper

INSTRUCTIONS

1. Remove glass from shadow box. Lightly sand all over to allow paint to adhere more easily to surface. Turn up metal pieces that held in glass and leave in the box as an accent.

2. Use foam brush to paint edges of shadow box, inside and out, in off-white acrylic. Allow to dry completely.

3. Loosely paint over off-white paint with brown, allowing some of the off-white to show through. Allow to dry completely.

4. Use glass from shadow box to measure paper. Cut paper slightly smaller than glass in order to fit into bottom of box. Glue into place with glue stick or spray adhesive.

5. Tear contrasting paper on top and cut into strip. Adhere to box with glue stick.

6. Tear pictures as shown and glue into shadow box.

7. Paint large chipboard "S" with off-white paint and let dry. Paint loosely with watered down pink paint. Dry completely. Tie on lace. Glue and staple on rick rack.

8. Apply all rub-ons.

9. Cut small picture and place behind pewter frame. Attach to box with foam tape.

10. Place wrought iron corner in position and secure with wood screws. Tuck in silk flowers as shown.

MY BABY
sIster

from ribbons and curls...

to heels and pearls...

all grown up

My Baby Sister
Diana Lyn McGraw

This is my gorgeous little sister, Charisse. I can't believe how much she has changed and grown over the years. It just seems like yesterday that she was busy playing with her Barbie dolls and watching "Little Mermaid" - and now she is all grown up with adult responsibilities. I think this shadow box reflects the changes and personal growth she has had over the years.

MATERIALS

Dye Inkpads: Tim Holz Black Soot Distress Ink by Ranger

Papers: Crate Paper

Markers/Pens: Black Zig Pen (05) by EK Success

Adhesives: Tacky Adhesive by 3M; Dimensional Dots by Therm O Web

Other: Shadow Box; Photo; Flowers by Teters and Prima Marketing; Alphabet Brads by Rusty Pickle; Letters and Chipboard by Heidi Swapp and Paper Studio; Tags by Crate Paper and Rusty Pickle; Ribbons

Tools: Dymo Labelmaker; Scissors; Sewing Machine

INSTRUCTIONS

1. Cut paper into three shapes: one rectangle and two trapezoids.
2. Cut circle shapes as shown. Ink all papers with Black Soot.
3. Adhere to white background paper and add photo.
4. Tie ribbons around mini circle tags and around hidden tag behind the photo.
5. Add title and flowers.
6. Add Dymo label at the top.
7. Sew along the edges of background paper three times.
8. Add brads in flower centers.
9. Adhere inked journal strips to complete.

CHAPTER 4 Altered Birdhouses

Red Robin Ranch Birdhouse
KC Willis

MATERIALS

Papers: Bird's Nest Paper (art supply store); Cardboard

Adhesives: Aleene's Tacky Glue by Duncan Enterprises

Other: Plain, Store-Bought Birdhouse and Wooden Bird; Buttons; Dowel; Rhinestones; Silk Flowers; Vintage Fabrics; Laces and Trims

Tools: Scissors; Marker; Drill and Drill Bit

INSTRUCTIONS

1. Arrange fabrics on birdhouse and adhere.

2. Make small collages on bird's nest paper with bits of paper, cardboard and fabric; adhere to birdhouse.

3. Drill a hole in top of bird house. Add dowel and wooden bird. Arrange silk clowers at base of bird.

4. Add sparkle with trims, rhinestones and buttons.

5. Add quote.

Here in Colorado, ranches often have very cool names. One of my favorites is near Wolf Creek Pass called "Bout Time Ranch." I wanted to name my birdhouses like the ranches and they presented an ideal canvas for embellishing with the supplies that make up a good part of my fabric art. Red Robin Ranch seemed a perfect name for a tall red birdhouse.

Birdello Birdhouse

KC Willis

MATERIALS

Papers: Bird's Nest Paper
(art supply store); Cardboard
Other: Plain, Store-Bought
Birdhouse; Buttons; Rhinestones;
Bits of Rust (Roof, Hearts, Door,
Wrought Iron Fleur De Lis Emblem);
Vintage Fabrics, Silk Flowers;
Laces and Trims
Adhesives: Aleene's Tacky Glue
by Duncan Enterprises
Tools: Scissors

INSTRUCTIONS

1. Add all rusty pieces in materials
   list to plain birdhouse.
2. Arrange fabrics on birdhouse and
   adhere.
3. Make small collages on bird's nest
   paper with bits of paper, cardboard
   and fabric; adhere to birdhouse.
3. Add sparkle with trims, lace, silk
   flowers, rhinestones and buttons.

When I was originally gathering up bits to embellish a few birdhouses, I found I had some vintage bright red trim from an old bedspread. I realized I had the perfect materials on hand to make one of the birdhouses a bit more garish - like a bordello. At first I thought it would be fun to call it "The Cathouse Birdhouse," but that was a little wordy. I love a play on words and the name "Birdello" seemed the ticket. It would take some truly sassy birds to call this one home.

When I am in my studio I always listen to music. I was working on this piece of artwork while listening to some of my favorite songs that really inspire me to stretch a step beyond my comfort zone. I love how this piece came together as it represents everything I believe in. When you are home you find comfort… comfort to dream, the ability to fly and the desire to soar toward your highest hopes.

$\mathcal{F}$ly, Soar, Dream

Kristen Robinson

MATERIALS

Foam Stamps: Swirls by Making Memories

Dye Inkpads: Memories Black by Stewart Superior

Papers: White Cardstock

Paints: Cream, Black, Blue, Gold and Red Acrylics

Stickers/Rub-Ons: BasicGrey

Adhesives: Craft Glue

Other: Small Wooden Box (with a removable lid); Charcoal Pencil; No. 2 Pencil; Gloss Gel Medium by Golden; Strip of Metal; Miniature Birds Nest; ½" x ½" Piece of Foam; Wire

Tools: Hammer and Nails; Paintbrush; Sandpaper; Glue Gun

INSTRUCTIONS

1. Remove lids from boxes and glue to the bottom or back of boxes. Once glue is dry, paint all boxes completely in desired acrylic paint color. Set them aside to dry.

2. Create three pieces of artwork at least 4" x 4" or use a piece that inspires you. Copy and print image, reducing it to 2" x 2". Seal with gel medium and let dry.

3. Stamp Swirls in black ink all over the outside of one box; let dry. Adhere paper to another box.

4. Sand all edges of the boxes, as well as stamped areas to create an aged appearance.

5. Glue foam to back of reduced artwork. Once sufficiently dry, glue the foam-mounted art into the opening of the boxes.

6. Use glue gun to attach bird nest to top of boxes or tile to front of birdhouse.

7. Bend strip of weathered metal in half and nail to boxes, being mindful of the metal's sharp edges. Sand metal to age.

8. Write inspirational words or messages in pencil around your artwork or if desired, adhere book page to frame in sections as shown. Lightly dry-brush with acrylic paints.

9. Insert a wire hook through the metal at the top to finish.

Nest
Kristen Robinson

MATERIALS

Papers: Discarded Book Pages
Paints: Cream and Brown Acrylic by Golden
Adhesives: Gel Medium by Golden
Other: Birdhouse; Pheasant Feathers; Glass Pebble; Charm; 20-Gauge Copper Wire; Twigs; Fiber; Tea-Dyed String; Walnut Ink (in spray bottle) by Tsukineko
Tools: Glue Gun; Needle Nose Pliers; Wire Cutters; Paintbrush; Sandpaper

INSTRUCTIONS

1. Paint entire birdhouse with cream acrylic, set aside to dry.

2. Using discarded book pages (preferably not too thick), tear random strips. Once birdhouse is dry, apply the strips with gel medium; let dry.

3. Randomly spray water onto the paper. Use your finger to roll portions of the paper away so the other side of the page shows through, creating a transfer.

4. Once the water has dried, go back over all the paper and birdhouse with brown acrylic paint; set aside to dry.

5. Sand all the edges as well as portions of the paper.

6. Gather feathers and twigs together and wrap with wire and tea-dyed string. Glue into onto the front of birdhouse using a hot glue gun.

7. Once glue has dried, wrap copper wire around birdhouse in a random fashion as shown.

8. Randomly crimp wire with needle nose pliers to create movement.

9. Add more strips of paper at the top to resemble a nest, adding a feather and twig for dimension.

10. Use a hot glue gun to add twigs at the base of birdhouse as well as randomly placed fiber.

11. In the center below the roof, apply a glass pebble charm.

12. Finally, stand about a foot away from the piece and randomly spray it with walnut ink.

This time of year I find myself wandering back to the memories of my pregnancy with my son. I recollect special moments, particularly how awed I was by the fact domestication hit me full force. The need and desire to nest, if you will, came a little unexpectedly. I reveled in cleaning, preparing and just being in the moment when at home. This piece is not the norm for me as it includes many natural and basic elements; however, it truly is a reflection of the impact that motherhood, especially pregnancy, had on my life.

This project came about as a result of a shopping trip with my Mum. She is a keen bird watcher and likes to do what she can to encourage birds to come into her garden. There were various types of birdhouses for sale and it made me wonder how or even if birds think about what style house to nest in. I suspect they just seek somewhere safe, and the aesthetics has more to do with what we like to look at!

Always on the lookout for interesting "stuff" to alter and or decorate, I decided to buy a couple of different shapes of birdhouses to use as a starting point for other projects. My husband says that I put way too much thought into these things and that it's just an excuse for me to play around with "stuff" - he may be right!

Home Sweet Home
Sue Roddis

MATERIALS

Rubber Stamps: Ledger Border, Wordy Woman and Newsy Bird by Stampers Anonymous

Dye Inkpads: Black by Memories

Papers: Brown Corrugated Cardstock; White Cardstock

Paints: Aleene's Premium Coat Bubble Gum Pink and Burnt Umber by Duncan Enterprises; Mauve Acrylic Glaze by Golden; White Gesso

Adhesives: Polyvinyl Acetate (PVA)

Other: Wooden Bird Nesting Box; Small Wooden Hearts; Small Glass Mosaic Tiles; Letter Beads; Thin White Sheer Ribbon; Scrabble-Style Alphabet Squares; Rusty Metal Bird Shape; Paper Flowers; Plastic Coated Wire Garden Mesh; Paper Alphabet Letters

Tools: Stapler; Paintbrush; Old Credit Card

INSTRUCTIONS

1. Roughly paint the birdhouse with gesso, set aside to dry. Use a paper towel to rub on mauve glaze. Set aside to dry again.

2. Paint several pieces of corrugated cardstock with a mixture of pink and brown paint; add gesso for white highlights on some of the ridges. Set aside to dry. Tear and cut the corrugated cardstock into pieces and glue these to the birdhouse as shown.

3. Color several pieces of white cardstock with a mixture of the pink and brown paints. A creative way to do this is to place small drops of each color along one edge of the cardstock and then use an old credit card to push and pull the paint across the card.

4. When the painted cardstock is dry, stamp it with several Newsy Bird, Wordy Woman and Ledger Border images and then cut them out.

5. Glue the ledger border pieces to the roof of the birdhouse as roof tiles.

6. Glue a row of small mosaic tiles to the front and back edges of the roof.

7. Wrap several paper flowers together and then glue them down the front of the birdhouse; add a cut out leaf stem and a piece of plastic garden mesh to the bottom.

8. Glue several bird images around the roof.

9. Spell out "home sweet home", using different styles of letter beads for each word. Thread the beads onto lengths of thin sheer ribbon and staple to front of birdhouse.

10. Add painted wooden hearts to the front as shown.

11. Decorate the sides with women, bird images and scrabble-style alphabet squares.

12. For the back, adhere a rusty metal bird shape, a couple of paper flowers and paper alphabet letters spelling "home sweet home".

Home is Where the Heart is

Sue Roddis

MATERIALS

Rubber Stamps: Home, Dymo Numbers and Love by Paperbag Studios; Printer's Lowercase Alphabet by Hero Arts

Dye Inkpads: Memories Black by Stewart Superior

Papers: Green 12"x12" Cardstock by Bazzill Basics; Ochre, White and Corrugated Cardstock; White Tissue Paper

Paints: Aleene's Premium Coat Yellow Ochre by Duncan Enterprises; White Gesso

Adhesives: Polyvinyl Acetate (PVA); JudiKins Diamond Glaze; Foam Sticky Pads

Other: Wooden Bird Nesting Box; Hexagonal Papier Mache Box; Small Wooden Heart Box; Wire; Leaf Beads; Plastic Hearts; Metal Screw Ring; Jump Rings; Brass Keyhole and Key Charms; Wooden Hearts; Scrabble-Style Alphabet Squares

Tools: Dymo Labelmaker; Heart Punch; Paintbrush; Scissors

INSTRUCTIONS

1. Paint the birdhouse, paper mache box and heart box with white gesso and set aside to dry.

2. Cut strips of cardstock to fit around the body of the birdhouse. Paint them randomly with Yellow Ochre paint and patches of gesso. Allow to dry and glue in place.

3. Stamp the home image in black onto ochre cardstock. Stamp enough times to fit around the birdhouse and cut out each piece. Repeat the process on white cardstock. Cut out the small house-shaped images and glue them over the corresponding images on the ochre cardstock. Glue the images around the birdhouse.

4. For the roof of the house, cut pieces of corrugated cardstock to fit and glue them in place. Add a little color with an almost dry paint brush dipped in very little paint. Paint three wooden hearts with Yellow Ochre paint; use a black inkpad to add highlights. Use a Dymo machine to print the words, "home is where the heart is" onto a paper strip. Color the strip with a little paint or ink and glue the words to the hearts; glue the hearts to the roof.

5. Use alphabet stamps to stamp the words, "home" and "heart" onto two plastic hearts. Make two wire plants for the front of the house by threading a plastic heart onto the middle of a length of wire. Twist to make a short stem and then add a leaf bead, twist the wire again to make a short side stem. Add further leaf beads and keep twisting to achieve the length you need.

6. Cut plant pot shapes from corrugated cardstock, attach the wire plants to the front of the house and add the plant pots over them to hide the ends of wire.

7. Screw a small metal ring above the entrance to the birdhouse and from it hang a brass keyhole and key charms with jump rings.

continued...

Home is Where the Heart is
continued

This birdhouse project also came about as a result of that same shopping trip with my Mum for a birdhouse for her garden. Once this one was decorated, although I liked the way it turned out, I felt it was missing something. So I set it aside for awhile hoping something would come to me! While looking through a cupboard, I happened upon a hexagonal papier mache box I had previously purchased and thought, "I wonder if the birdhouse will fit on here?" I tried it, it did and it looked good... I found what it needed!

8. Paint the paper mache box randomly with Yellow Ochre paint so some gesso is still visible.

9. Stamp the Dymo numbers image several times onto white tissue paper. Cut out the images and use Diamond Glaze to apply them around the sides of the box lid. The Glaze will make the tissue seem to disappear and the images will look as if they are stamped directly onto the box.

10. Use scrabble alphabet tiles to add the words, "home is where the heart is" around the sides of the box base.

11. Paint the inside of the box as before and use the tissue method to apply stamped heart images (from the Love stamp) around the inside.

12. Paint the small wooden heart box with Yellow Ochre paint. When dry, rub a black inkpad around the edges. Use the tissue and Diamond Glaze method to add Dymo numbers around the sides and a heart image to the top. Place the heart box inside the larger paper mache box.

13. Glue the birdhouse to the top of the paper mache box.

So, I decorated the box to match the house and glued it in place. Again, I set it aside thinking it was done. Then while out shopping I saw the small wooden heart box. I bought it knowing just where it would fit. So once again I was back to work decorating it to match the rest of the project. I think it fits in perfectly with the "home is where the heart is" theme... although my husband now thinks my heart lives in a box - but never mind - he doesn't "get it" every time!!!

Sweetheart
Audrey Hernandez

MATERIALS

Papers: K&Company
Paints: Spotlight by Making Memories
Adhesives: Mod Podge by Plaid
Stickers/Rub-Ons: Stickers by K&Company;
Rub-Ons by American Traditional Designs
Other: Heart Brad by Creative Impressions; Old
Book Page; Ribbons by Offray; Wooden Heart
Tools: Dremel or Drill with Small Drill Bit

INSTRUCTIONS

1. Adhere paper and old book page to wooden heart using Mod Podge.
2. Rub a little paint over top and bottom.
3. Add sticker and brad to top middle and add "p.s." sticker to bottom.
4. Add birds and word rub-ons.
5. Adhere ribbon to sides of wooden heart, make holes at top of heart and tie ribbon through to hang.

These two little birds look like they are just smitten with each other, so I had to create something around a love theme. All the elements just came together for this one so easily... the postage stamp, the word rub-ons and the "p.s." at the tail end, as if there were one more thing but unknown to us.

Naturally Beautiful
Audrey Hernandez

When I saw this little girl with her pail it reminded me of the ocean and its beauty. We live only a few minutes from the beach so it is one of my favorite themes to work with. I made sure to use some sunny, fun, and warm colors just the way the beach is on a beautiful day.

MATERIALS

Rubber Stamps: Paperbag Studios

Dye Inkpads: StazOn Jet Black by Tsukeniko

Papers: Daisy D's Paper Co.

Stickers/Rub-Ons: Postage Sticker and "naturally beautiful" by K&Company

Adhesives: Mod Podge by Plaid; Glue Stick

Other: Stars; Collage Image by PaperWhimsy; Flower; Ribbon; Old Book Page; Wooden Heart

Tools: Dremel or Drill with Small Drill Bit

INSTRUCTIONS

1. Use Mod Podge to cover wooden heart with old book page and patterned paper.
2. Overstamp in black ink.
3. Add brad to the flower and flower to the wooden heart as shown.
4. Adhere collage image, stars, sticker and "naturally beautiful" words.
5. Edge the sides of heart with ribbon.
6. Make holes at top of heart and tie ribbon through to hang.

Butterfly Home
Audrey Hernandez

MATERIALS

Rubber Stamps: Paperbag Studios

Dye Inkpads: StazOn Jet Black by Tsukineko

Papers: NRN Designs; The Paper Company

Pastels/Chalks: Portfolio Series Water Soluble Oil Pastels by Binney & Smith

Adhesives: Mod Podge by Plaid; Glue Stick

Other: Collage Image; Butterfly and Egg by PaperWhimsy; Mini Clips by Karen Foster Design; Decorative Wallpaper; Ribbon; Wooden Heart

Tools: Dremel or Drill with Small Drill Bit

INSTRUCTIONS

1. Adhere patterned papers to wooden heart.
2. Overstamp in black ink.
3. Add flower, then girl image and then two pieces of wallpaper to make roof of house.
4. Outline image with black oil pastel.
5. Add butterfly, clip and egg.
6. Add ribbon to sides of heart then make two holes at top to thread ribbon through.

One Little Indian

Audrey Hernandez

MATERIALS

Rubber Stamps: Sunday International
Dye Inkpads: StazOn Jet Black by Tsukineko
Papers: BasicGrey; Scenic Route Paper Company
Paints: Spotlight by Making Memories
Adhesives: Mod Podge by Plaid; Glue Stick
Other: Collage Image by ARTchix Studio; Flower Punches; Dymo Labelmaker; Old Book Page; Wooden Heart
Tools: Dremel or Drill with Small Drill Bit

INSTRUCTIONS

1. Adhere papers to wooden heart.
2. Randomly smear on a little white paint.
3. Stamp barbed wire and sunburst.
4. Make title with Dynamo Labelmaker
5. Add collage image, flower punches and title.
6. Make holes at top and tie ribbon through; edge sides of heart with ribbon.

Another piece inspired by my wee one. This little Indian is just standing there so strong and tough in all his cuteness. I wanted to use some nice colors to evoke this and also loved the addition of the barbed wire to make the piece come together.

As you'll see with most of my art, I love the "home" theme. This little girl deserved a house of her own with all of nature surrounding her.

MATERIALS

Markers/Pens: Fine Point Marker by Sharpie

Papers: Birds Nest Paper (art supply store); Corrugated Cardboard Scraps

Adhesives: Craft Glue

Other: Old Window; New and Vintage Coffee-Stained Fabrics, Embellishments and Hat Flowers; Old Photos; Heavy-Weight and Coffee-Stained Canvas; Photo Transfer Paper by Avery; Pom-Pom Trim

Tools: Iron; Needle and Thread; Hammer and Nails; Saw; Heat Gun

I purchased this old window with its original chippy paint at a farmhouse auction. I added the ledge just for fun and bought new glass panes.

Fallen Angels Altered Window Pane
KC Willis

INSTRUCTIONS

1. Cut a piece of plywood to fit behind the glass pane area.

2. Select fabrics, tear to size and sew around the edges.

3. Glue fabrics to plywood.

4. Select images and print on transfer paper following manufacturer's instructions. Apply to fabric with iron.

5. Sew around edges of pictures and glue to papers that have been torn to size and burned around the edges.

6. Write quotes to correspond with photos.

7. Glue images and quotes to fabric-covered plywood, keeping in mind where your panes will be.

8. Trim top border with pom-poms.

9. Embellish using bits and pieces that will fit behind glass.

10. Drop glass into window pane area.

11. Hammer plywood very carefully onto window edges.

Celebrate Life in the Round

Kristen Robinson

I instantly fell in love with the new stamps from Paper Bag Studios and knew they deserved to be used in a unique way. After stumbling across this bowl in a department store, I had a light bulb moment to create a collage in the center of it. The idea to create a circular frame with depth really appealed to me. It reminded me of those Easter eggs we used to receive as kids; the eggs that reveal an entire tableau once you dare to look inside and steal a peak. I wanted this bowl to be a bit like that on a large scale with perhaps a little less secretiveness about it.

MATERIALS

Rubber Stamps: Be Happy, Daisy and 1937 Post by Paperbag Studios; Celebrate by Stampin' Up

Dye Inkpads: Tim Holtz Brushed Corduroy Distress Ink and Vermillion Lacquer by Ranger

Papers: Red Floral, Cream and Red Polka Dots and Ledger Paper by Making Memories; Stamped Ledger Paper (source unknown)

Paints: Red and Cream Acrylic

Colored Pencils: Prismacolor Scarlet Lake by Sanford

Adhesives: Craft Glue

Other: Wooden Bowl; Cream Velvet Ribbon; Gel Medium; Gloss Varnish (water-based) Masking Tape

Tools: Paper Trimmer; Xacto Knife; Paintbrush; Deco Shears

INSTRUCTIONS

1. Use the bottom of the bowl as a template and create a circle on the back of the stamped ledger paper; cut out.

2. Use masking tape to mask off an even number of stripes on the outside of the bowl.

3. Paint exposed stripes on bowl with cream acrylic paint, let dry.

4. Remove masking tape and fill in the remaining area with red acrylic paint.

5. Randomly stamp the ledger paper circle with small font phrase in Vermillion Lacquer. Add scribbles with colored pencil. Ink the outside edges with Brushed Corduroy and let dry.

6. Use pinking edge of deco shears to cut a square from red polka dot paper. Ink edges with Brushed Corduroy.

7. Cut a slightly small square from red floral paper. Ink edges with Brushed Corduroy. Layer to polka dot paper.

8. Stamp Be Happy in Brushed Corduroy on plain ledger paper. Tear a small amount from the bottom of panel. Add highlights around the stamp with the Scarlet Lake colored pencil. Layer to papers.

9. Stamp the word "celebrate" in Brushed Corduroy ink on a smaller scrap of ledger paper. Ink edges and add a few lines with colored pencil.

10. Mount square collage onto the center of stamped ledger paper. Brush on a thin coat of gel medium. Remove bubbles, being careful not to smear the ink by rubbing too hard.

11. Coat the bowl inside and out with varnish (avoid the bottom). Let dry completely.

12. Spread a thick coating of gel medium into the bottom of the bowl, add collage and smooth with bone folder. Let dry.

13. Adhere cream velvet ribbon to bottom of bowl if you desire to hang on wall.

15. Once completely dry, hang or use practically anywhere as a great looking accessory.

Red is not a color I use often, believe it or not, I am actually a little afraid of it. However, I figured if I was literally jumping out of the box I might as well dislodge myself from my comfort zone and pull out all the stops. I encourage you to jump outside yours and find something funky in which to create a collage. You never know what you might end up with.

I got some little half wooden eggs from the craft store and immediately knew that I wanted to do some kind of nature theme. The nest and bird from Cavallini & Co. were perfect additions. I love nature and life, I always think what a miracle it all is, so this piece just makes me happy every time I see it.

Roots

Audrey Hernandez

MATERIALS:

Rubber Stamps: Paperbag Studios

Dye Inkpads: StazOn Jet Black by Tsukineko

Papers: Daisy D's Paper Co.

Paints: FolkArt Metallic Antique Copper by Plaid

Stickers/Rub-Ons: Heart Sticker by Creative Imaginations; Rub-Ons by American Traditional Designs and Junkitz

Adhesives: Gel Medium by Golden

Other: Screen Covers and Rusty Tin Heart by DCC Crafts; Wooden Eggs by Lara's Crafts; Swirl Leaf by FoofaLa; Girl Image by PaperWhimsy; Bird and Nest by Cavallini & Co.; Flowers by Prima Marketing; Miracle of Nature by K&Company; Gems by Making Memories; Ribbon; Old Book Pages

Tools: Paintbrush; Hole Punch

INSTRUCTIONS

1. Paint both metal screen frames with metallic antique copper.

2. Add rub-ons to front and inside perimeters on metal screen panels.

3. Adhere papers, heart, leaf and rub-ons to front of screen.

4. Paint wooden eggs and attach in a row to front of screen at bottom.

5. Adhere papers, girl, nest, flowers, gems and words to left inside screen panel.

6. Adhere papers, bird, heart sticker and flower to right inside screen panel. Stamp numbers in black.

7. Punch holes through screens and tie together with ribbon.

She Who Is My Daughter
Altered Suitcase *Cathy Lucas*

MATERIALS

Rubber Stamps: Aloha Alphabet ("She") and Toscana by Rusty Pickle; Forever by Heidi Swapp

Papers: Vintage Heirloom Collection by Rusty Pickle; Black Cardstock

Paints: Black Acrylic by Plaid

Markers/Pens: Zig Memory System White Chalk Marker by EK Success

Stickers/Rub-Ons: Black Rub-Ons by Making Memories

Adhesives: Polyvinyl Acetate (PVA); Double-Sided Tape; Glue Dots; Pop-Up Glue Dots

Other: Small Cardboard Suitcase (from Ross); Foam Board by Magic Scraps; Bookbinding Tape by Making Memories; Flowers by Prima Marketing; Ribbons; Fabrics; Fibers; Antique Tags; Chipboard Alphabet Letters and Chipboard Frame and Tags by Rusty Pickle; White Clothes Hook; Small Black and Large Silver Brads; Buttons; Magnetic Words; Shell Bracelet; Word Dog Tags; Velcro Tabs; Black File Folder

Tools: Flower Punch by EK Success; Sandpaper; Small Foam Paintbrush; Anywhere Hole Punch; Scissors; Ruler; Paper Cutter

INSTRUCTIONS

OUTSIDE OF CASE:

1. If possible, remove handle from case and set aside.

2. Lightly sand box inside and out. Wipe clean.

3. Use back of box as a template and trace outline on foam board. Cut out foam board on the inside of line so it is slightly smaller than the box. Set aside.

4. Adhere pieced pattered paper to front, sides and back of box so that the outside is covered.

5. Stamp with "She" and Toscana images on the front of the case using black acrylic paint.

6. Distress edges as desired with black acrylic paint; let dry.

7. If you removed the handle, replace it now. Secure with large brads.

INSIDE OF CASE:

1. Adhere patterned paper to foam board and foam board to the back of the case.

2. Glue pieced patterned paper to the lid of the case.

3. Adhere black cardstock around the top, side and bottom of case.

4. Use black acrylic paint to carefully paint around the edge between the cardstock and the foam board. Let dry.

5. Reinforce area between the lid and the case with bookbinding tape.

6. Attach clothes hook to side of case using the anywhere hole punch; mount with small screws or brads and Tacky Tape.

7. Hang bracelet, dog tags and brown string from hook. Secure with tape.

8. Mount photo to black cardstock that is ½" larger than the photo. Apply decorative trim to left side of photo. Punch holes in chipboard photo corner and tie with ribbon. Adhere to top right corner with tape.

9. Paint chipboard letters "She" and outline letters with white chalk marker. Let dry. Adhere to the back of case with pop-up glue dots. Use glue dots to secure ribbon knots to the letters.

10. Attach fabric knot to the hook.

11. Adhere fiber to bottom of case for texture.

   continued...

She Who Is My Daughter Altered Suitcase
continued

INSIDE OF LID:

1. Paint the lip of the case with black acrylic paint. Let dry.
2. Stamp "forever" with black acrylic paint on one of the antique tags; let dry. Tape to lid.
3. Wrap and tape and two antique tags from the back of the black file folder so they meet in the front.
4. Tie the tags in the middle with ribbon.
5. Using rub-ons, stamps or your own handwriting, place "who is my" on the left side tag and "Daughter" on the right side tag.
6. Punch out four flowers, layer together with Prima flowers to make two flowers and adhere to tags with black brads. Attach to tags.
7. Journal on the inside of file folder.
8. Decorate the lid with magnetic words, buttons, chipboard letters, word stickers… whatever! This is where you make your shadow box "speak" about your subject.
9. Secure Velcro where the file folder is placed.

FINISHING TOUCHES:

1. Adhere fabric to the outside lip of the lid.
2. Tie desired amount of ribbon, fabric and fiber to the handle of the suitcase.
3. Punch out flowers and place them over the screws or brads on the outside of the case.

*G*arden of My Heart Altered Dress Form

Teemie Eschenburg

MATERIALS

Rubber Stamps: Penny Black; Stampers Anonymous; Fine Line Classics by Inkadinkado

Dye Inkpads: Archival Sepia, Adirondack Lettuce and Butterscotch Color Wash by Ranger

Papers: Parchment; Rose Paper by Daisy D's Paper Co.; Contrasting Paper

Paints: Acrylic

Adhesives: Aleene's Tacky Glue by Duncan Enterprises; Hot Melt Glue Pot

Other: Preassembled Dress Form and Stand; Vintage Fabrics Pieces; Laces; Buttons; Assorted Trims; Random Finds; Various Ribbons (10 yards); Bees Wax; Gold Leaf; Tags; DMC Pearle Cotton Thread; Dried Herbs and Pansies

Tools: Glue Gun; Paintbrush; Needle; Scissors; Pencil; Serrated Knife; Awl; Popsicle Stick

*N*eedle in hand at three years old, I learned how to allow my creative energies to flow at a young age. Loved by two talented grandmothers, one taught the disciplined way of needle arts and machine- and hand-sewing, the other taught the freedom of ribbon and fancy fiber arts.

Both Grandmothers had a love for nature. Cabbage roses, real and fabric, along with flower and herb gardens have always been a part of my life, inspiring my creativity to lean towards the celebration of God's earthly blessings.

continued...

Inside Front

INSTRUCTIONS

1. Use pencil to draw a heart shape on the front and back of the form. Cut out front heart carefully with serrated knife, be careful not to cut all the way through the form. Paint dress form and heart shape inside and out with acrylic paint to prime. Set aside to dry.

2. Tear the rose paper around the large flowers, and tear a sheet of contrasting paper.

3. Make a paste/dye blend with glue and butterscotch color wash. Add enough water to create the thickness of heavy cream; stir well with popsicle stick.

4. Dip the torn paper into the mixture and allow to soak for 30 seconds; lift out and drain off excess. Begin applying from top of form to bottom. Cover entire outside of form, except the heart shape. Apply contrast paper to heart shape and to the heart outline on the inside of the form. Allow to dry.

5. Computer-generate the words, "garden of my heart" and print onto parchment paper.

6. Glue gold leaf to inside of heart along with the printed words. Use awl to carefully punch holes through both form and heart in order to lace ribbons later. Punch three holes on each left side and one on each right.

7. Spray tags with dye, allow to dry. Stamp randomly with words. Once dry, use bees wax to place random finds on one side of the circle tags.

8. Create roses and leaves with various ribbons; hand-stitch to hold shape until glued in place with hot glue. Embellish inside of form as you wish.

9. Affix dried pansies with bees wax. Stamp dress form randomly. Glue vintage laces in place to create the bustle. Add vintage finds, buttons, ribbon roses and leaves. Embellish top of form with gathers of lace, vintage ribbons roses and findings. Lace ribbons through the holes to attach the heart. Tie bows to secure.

Inside Back

The crosses are made from scraps of fence boards that I collect from my neighborhood whenever anyone tears down an old fence. They are cut and nailed together. In some cases, as in this one, they are whitewashed with diluted house paint.

The Guadalupe Cross   *KC Willis*

MATERIALS

Papers: Bird's Nest Paper (art supply store); Cardboard

Paints: White House Paint by Behr

Adhesives: Aleene's Tacky Glue by Duncan Enterprises

Other: Plain, Store-Bought Birdhouse; Rhinestone Button; Gold Doily; Scraps of Old Fence Boards (or wood strips); Vintage Image; Vintage Fabrics, Laces and Trims

Tools: Scissors; Saw; Hammer and Nails

INSTRUCTIONS

1. Saw fence boards and nail together to create crosses; whitewash with diluted house paint and allow to dry.
2. Transfer vintage image to fabric.
3. Stitch around transferred image. Layer onto bird nest and cardboard.
4. Adhere fabric to cross. Embellish with laces, trims, gold doily and rhinestone button.
5. Glue prepared vintage image transfer to center of cross.

I have always loved crosses. I collect them, as a matter of fact. The idea of taking the smooth, blank canvas of wood pieces and giving them texture by adding fabrics and trims pleases me. I sometimes put the image of strong women of the west on my crosses, but on this one I chose to keep the original spirituality intact and add a Guadalupe. The gold doily and rhinestone button were added to give it the look of the inside of an ornate Catholic church.

Postcard Standup Figures
Lou McCulloch

MATERIALS

Papers: Matte Photo Paper by Epson

Markers/Pens: Black Permanent Marker by Sharpie

Colored Pencils: White

Pastels/Chalks: Portfolio Series Oil Pastels by Binney & Smith

Adhesives: JudiKins Diamond Glaze; Multipurpose Adhesive Spray by 3M; Matte Sealer Spray by Plaid

Other: Colorful Vintage Postcards of Figures; Tags; Word Beads by Collage Keepsakes; Red Heart Brads by Creative Impressions; Raffia; Black Foam Board (3/16" thick)

Tools: Mat Cutter; Scissors

I have always collected colorful vintage postcards because I enjoy their frivolity. They remind of a time when postcards could be sent through the mail on short notice and messages frequently indicated a meeting the next day. I wanted to have some of these vivid, large figures on my shelf and decided to enlarge some images. I added the bead words as embellishments and as themes to each piece. I gave one figure with a personal sentiment as a gift to a friend for her birthday. At Christmas, I always set up a display of holiday stand-ups for a striking arrangement.

INSTRUCTIONS

1. Copy and enlarge postcard figures onto matte photo paper, printing as large as possible. Cut out, leaving a base for the figure to stand. Highlight the edges of the images with Portfolio Series Oil Pastels. Spray with matte sealer in even coats and allow to dry.

2. Place cutout on black foam board and trace with white colored pencil. Use mat cutter to carefully cut out the figures by following the white lines. Set aside.

3. Lightly spray the back of the cutout and the top of the foam board with adhesive. After ten seconds, carefully position the postcard figure over the foam board cutout, aligning all edges. You will have up to 30 seconds to reposition. Touch up the edges with black marker.

4. To make a stand, attach a small block of foam board, approximately 1 ½" by 2 ½" to the bottom reverse. Cut a groove in the center with mat cutter and add a triangle of foam board to form a stand. You may have to try a few shapes to get the right angle for your figure to stand. Once you are pleased with the result, glue in place with Diamond Glaze.

5. Attach word beads with glaze on front to form sayings, or if making a clown, place a dot of glaze on heart brads and push into foam to form buttons. Tie a colorful tag with raffia if desired.

6. Make a grouping of these figures as a holiday display or to place on your shelf for inspiration.

MATERIALS

Dye Inkpads: Tim Holtz Black Soot and Brushed Corduroy by Ranger
Papers: Ledger Paper; Distressed Dots; White and Red Cardstock
Paints: Cream, Rust and Black
Adhesives: Craft Glue; Masking Tape

Other: 12" Peg Shelf; Vintage Photos; 24-Gauge Copper Wire; Twigs; Twine; Small Metal Key; Copper Aging Solution; Paper Towels; Pencil

Tools: Glue Gun; Scissors; Wire Cutters; Pliers; Paintbrush

Family Tree
Kristen Robinson

I am fascinated by the idea of mail order brides and arranged marriages in the 1800's. When I came across the photo of this young woman I found myself contemplating her life. Did she marry for love, was she a mail order bride or did she simply marry to please her family? The idea of two people coming together, creating a home and a family tree is a common theme in my artwork. I feel this assemblage conveys the journey we take, the people we discover and the experiences we acquire while on the path of life.

INSTRUCTIONS

1. Remove pegs from holes of shelf; use pliers if necessary.

2. Paint shelf and pegs with cream paint. Set aside to dry.

3. Streak wood with rust paint. I used a paper towel to randomly dab on the color for an aged appearance. Allow to dry.

4. Use a paper towel to rub on black paint. Set aside to dry completely.

5. Choose a vintage photo of a woman and a man and copy each onto heavy cardstock. Cut them out to create two figures.

6. Make a heart out of red cardstock and ink the edges. Glue a piece of twine to the back of the heart and let dry.

7. Glue heart onto hands of vintage woman.

8. Tie a piece of twine onto the top of a metal key. Glue this onto the hand of the vintage man so he appears to be holding it.

9. Glue the figures onto the pegs you removed from the shelf. It is important to use a glue gun or another form of aggressive glue.

10. Cut a square from the ledger paper for a house. Create a roof with distressed dot paper and adhere to the square. Highlight the structure with pencil.

11. Place the word "Dream" on the front of the house. Glue house to peg and set aside to dry.

12. Bunch together various sizes of twigs. Secure them with a small piece of masking tape and glue to peg.

13. Tightly wrap copper wire around the twigs to cover all of the tape and to secure the twigs a bit more to the peg. (You may optionally first dip the wire into copper aging solution to dull the shine.)

14. Add a layer of twine for dimension.

15. Create small tags from ledger paper to hang from the twigs. Ink the edges with brushed corduroy. Computer-generate your favorite words or phrases that have to do with family or home and adhere to tags. Add a small piece of wire to the back of each tag to help remain upright when placed on the tree.

16. Wrap tags onto twigs with copper wire.

17. Now place the figures, artwork and tree back into the peg holes. If you would like to permanently secure the figures, place a small dot of hot glue into the peg holes and let dry.

18. Randomly glue twigs around figures to add a bit more dimension.

have made dozens of these bowls and used them for gift containers. I fill them with movie tickets and candy bars or DVDs and ready-to-pop popcorn. (Although the Elmer's Glue is nontoxic, the bowl is not intended for unwrapped food or liquids.)

Ticket Bowl

Ginny Carter Smallenburg

MATERIALS

Papers: Marilyn Monroe Wrapping Paper (source unknown)
Adhesives: Elmer's School Glue
Other: Ticket Roll (office supply); Glass and Metal Frame; Ball Chain (craft store)
Tools: Paintbrush; Drill

INSTRUCTIONS

1. Using your thumbs, press the center of the ticket roll gently, while rotating the roll. Keep pressing and rotating, moving your thumbs higher and higher towards the top edge. The amount of pressure and the tightness of the original ticket roll will determine the shape of the finished bowl. If you are not happy with the shape, press the roll back into the starting roll. The bottom may be flattened out by gently tapping it onto a flat surface.

2. Use a paintbrush to coat the entire bowl inside and out with Elmer's Glue. Let dry thoroughly. The glue will dry clear. You could also use matte or gloss medium, but the glue is less expensive and works great.

3. The frame and glass come in coordinating sizes. Just add an image. Drill a small hole and attached the frame with a ball chain.

La Femme Collaged Vintage Bottles

Lindsay Haglund

MATERIALS

Papers: Scrapbook & Collage Papers ~ The European Collection by TweetyJill Publications

Adhesives: Yes! Paste by Gane Brothers & Lane; E-6000 by Eclectic Products

Rubber Stamps: Cavallini & Co.

Other: Corked Vintage Bottles; Lace Trim; Ribbon; Metal Embellishment; Tags; Wax

Tools: Foam Brush; Scissors; Pinking Shears

INSTRUCTIONS

1. Cut out and trim desired papers and ephemera.
2. Use Yes! Paste and foam brush to apply papers to bottles.
3. Once dry, attach metal piece with E-6000. Allow to dry.
4. Cork bottle and dip into melted wax to seal.
5. Stamp tags and slip over top of bottle.
6. Tie on lace or ribbon as shown.

I like to make my gifts for family and friends when I have time. Collaged vintage bottles in interesting shapes make fabulous handmade gifts year round.

Fill with bath salts, bubble bath, bath oils and more. Consider homemade vinegars, sauces or drink mixes and decorate the outside to match the theme.

For a finished seal, hold upside down and dip the top in melted wax before tying on tags, ribbon or lace.

MATERIALS

Rubberstamps: Alphabet; Days of the Week; Small Font Stamp

Pigment Inkpads: VersaFine Onyx Black by Tsukineko; Various Colors of Ink

Papers: Ruler Paper by 7gypsies; Game Board Ephemera Paper from Collage & Scrapbook Papers ~ The French Collection by TweetyJill Publications

Paints: Titan Buff Acrylic and Gesso by Golden

Adhesives: Yes! Paste by Gane Brothers & Lane or Matte Gel Medium by Golden; E-6000 by Eclectic Products

Other: Clipboard; Metal Label Holder with Brads; Antique Ruler Pieces; Vintage Photos; Computer-Generated Phrase; Coin Holder; Ephemera (P and C); Corrugated Cardstock

Tools: Paintbrush

Passages Altered Clipboard

Joey Long

INSTRUCTIONS

1. Tear and cut desired papers, photos and ephemera to collage the clipboard. Set aside.

2. Paint gesso on front side of clipboard. Allow to dry.

3. Adhere papers and game board ephemera. Layer part of the photos as shown.

4. Dry-brush clipboard with Titan Buff acrylic paint. Allow to dry.

5. Rub colored inks onto coin holder, stamp with small font stamp and adhere over photo of standing man. Add phrase and bottom photo.

6. Stamp days of the week and passages.

7. Attach three-dimensional vintage ruler pieces with E-6000.

8. If desired, dry-brush a small amount of Titan Buff paint once more on the project as shown.

My father's parents died when he was quite young. He finished his childhood in an orphanage in Philadelphia. So much of his history is lost; I've chosen to augment family photos with relatives "acquired" from estate sales and flea markets. I take comfort in knowing that in some small way, I'm honoring these lost souls too. How did their family loose these precious photos?

My Blue Dress
Lou McCulloch

MATERIALS

Fabrics: Vintage Quilt Squares; Strips from Rag Ball; Fabric Alphabet Book; Inkjet Fabric Sheet by June Tailor; Doll Dress

Dye Inkpads: Tim Holtz Vintage Photo Distress Ink by Ranger

Other: Vintage Images; Four Small Red Buttons; Two Blue Buttons; Star Ribbon Trim; Mat Board; Frame (optional); Photo Editing Software

Tools: Serrated-Edge and Straight-Edge Scissors; Needle and Thread; Iron; Stapler

INSTRUCTIONS

1. Iron doll dress flat. Sew tiny buttons where desired, place a rag ball bow at the neck edge and fasten with thread.

2. Cut out a triangle from a vintage quilt square and sew star trim to top edge, leaving enough to form apron ties. The size of the triangle will depend on the size of the dress. Try the scrap of fabric around the waist before cutting to fit and adding the ties.

3. Cut letters from fabric alphabet book to form words. Short words such as "play", "girl", "kid" or "child" work well, but keep in mind there is only one letter to use in each word. Sew letters to the apron and randomly add a few buttons.

4. Use your photo software to print out images in blue onto the fabric photo sheets. Make sure you print on the rough fabric side. Cut out images with serrated-edge scissors. Run Distress Inkpad over edges and lightly touch the surface of the images to simulate age.

5. Scatter images over dress, small quilt squares, and apron and sew in place. I find that placing images at a slight angle makes a more pleasing arrangement.

6. Sew on two small quilt squares with images, making sure the images peek out from under the apron.

7. Staple dress to mat board and, if you wish, place in a frame. This makes a wonderful gift! You could even use the recipient's doll dress from childhood and add his or her own images to the dress and apron.

I purchased an old doll dress at a flea market and loved the soft shade of checkered blue in the pattern. I have many scraps of vintage quilt squares and thought the indigo blue patterned fabric went well with the dress. The fabric alphabet book was lying on the top of my fabric drawer and I thought that words from this would be easily sewn. I printed images of children from my photo collection in blue to complement the vintage clothes.

You can either find an old doll dress at a flea market, or use one from your childhood as a special remembrance.

After making this dress, I thought it would be a wonderful gift for my sister-in-law. Next year, for the holidays, I will print out images of her as a child, perhaps in sepia this time, and attach to a piece of vintage clothing. My quest this year will be to find an old brown doll dress!

This collage was done in postoid form...a sort of mini autobiography. My mother's engagement photo is the main image; the kangaroo with her 'joey'; the 50c is for the year of my birth; Zenobia is the name of a favorite childhood bear; the pen nib represents my years of calligraphic interest; the postmark is in French – I took 8 years of French in school! The heart sticker is similar to one my mother added to all her correspond...

You could use the same idea to create artist trading cards.

Photo Postoid of My Mother *Joey Long*

MATERIALS

Rubber Stamps: Various (source unknown)
Dye Inkpads: Black
Papers: White Copy Paper
Adhesives: Glue Stick
Other: Scrapbook; Plastic Slide Mounts; Ephemera
Tools: Scissors

INSTRUCTIONS:

1. Copy focus photo and cut out.
2. Collage related ephemera. Adhere photo.
3. Stamp images onto collage. Use rub-on letters and numbers as shown. Set aside.
4. Create nine rectangles to fit letter size paper.
5. Copy, shrink and adhere collages to fit each rectangle.
6. Copy entire sheet.
7. Further reduce one collage to fit in a slide mount. Layer onto artwork.
8. Adhere to scrapbook for a unique and creative layout.

Product Resource Guide

3M / Scotch: www.scotchbrand.com

7gypsies: www.7gypsies.com

A Fistful of Stamps: www.fistfulofstamps.com

AccuCut: www.accucut.com

Acey Deucy: www.aceydeucy.com

Adobe: www.adobe.com

American Crafts: www.americancrafts.com

American Traditional Designs: www.americantraditional.com

Art Gone Wild & Friends: www.agwstamps.com

Art Impressions: www.artimpressions.com

Art Institute Glitter, Inc.: www.artglitter.com

ARTchix Studio: www.artchixstudio.com

BasicGrey: www.basicgrey.com

Bazzill Basics Paper: www.bazzillbasics.com

Beeswax: www.beeswaxrubberstamps.com

Behr: www.behr.com

Binney & Smith: www.portfolioseries.com

Cavallini & Co.: www.cavallini.com

Claudine Hellmuth: www.lazarstudiowerx.com

Clearsnap, Inc.: www.clearsnap.com

Coffee Break Design: www.coffeebreakdesign.com

Collage Keepsakes: www.collagekeepsakes.com

Color Textiles, Inc.: www.colortextiles.com

Craf-t Products: www.craft-tproducts.com

Craft Smart: Local Craft Store

Crafter's Pick: www.crafterspick.com

Crate Paper: www.cratepaper.com

Creative Imaginations: www.cigift.com

Creative Impressions: www.creativeimpressions.com

Creativity, Inc.: www.creativitycraftsinc.com

Daisy D's Paper Co: www.daisydspaper.com

Darice: www.darice.com

DCC: www.dcccrafts.com

DecoArt: www.decoart.com

Deja Views: www.dejaviews.com

Delphi: www.delphiglass.com

Delta: www.deltacrafts.com

DMC: www.dmc-usa.com

Dover Publications: www.doverpublications.com

Dremel: www.dremel.com

Duncan Enterprises: www.duncancrafts.com

Dymo: www.dymo.com

Eclectic Products: www.eclecticproducts.com

EK Success: www.eksuccess.com

Elmer's: www.elmers.com

Epson: www.epson.com

Fancifuls Inc.: www.fancifulsinc.com

FoofaLa: www.foofala.com; 1-800-588-6707

Gane Brothers & Lane, Inc.: www.ganebrothers.com

Golden Artist Colors, Inc.: www.goldenpaints.com

Goop: Local Hardware Store

Hampton Art LLC: www.hamptonart.com

Heidi Swapp: www.heidiswapp.com

Hero Arts: www.heroarts.com

Imagination Project: www.imaginationproject.com

Inkadinkado Rubber Stamps: www.inkadinkado.com

JudiKins: www.judikins.com

Junkitz: www.junkitz.com

K&Company: www.kandcompany.com

Karen Foster Design: www.karenfosterdesign.com

Karen Russell: www.karenrussell.typepad.com

KI Memories: www.kimemories.com

KK Originals: www.kkoriginals.com

Krazy Glue: www.krazyglue.com

Product Resource Guide
continued

Krylon: www.krylon.com

McGill Inc.: Local Craft Store

Ma Vinci's Reliquary: http://reliquary.cyberstampers.com

Making Memories: www.makingmemories.com

Marah Johnson: www.marah_johnson.typepad.com

May Arts: www.mayarts.com

me & my BIG ideas: www.meandmybigideas.com

Melissa Frances: www.melissafrances.com

Memories Complete: www.memoriescomplete.com

Michelle Ward: www.itsmysite.com/michelleward/

My Mind's Eye: www.mymindseye.com

Nick Bantock: www.nickbantock.com

NRN Designs: http://nrninvitations.com

Offray: www.offray.com

Oriental Trading Company: www.orientaltrading.com

Oxford Impressions: www.oxfordimpressions.com

Paper House Productions:
www.paperhouseproductions.com

Paper Studio: www.paperstudio.com

Paperbag Studios: www.paperbagstudios.com

PaperWhimsy: www.paperwhimsy.com

Penny Black Rubber Stamps: www.pennyblackinc.com

Plaid Enterprises, Inc.: www.plaidonline.com

Postmodern Design: 405-321-3176

Prima Marketing, Inc.: www.primamarketing.com

Prym Consumer USA, Inc.: www.dritz.com

PSX: www.psxstamps.com

Ranger Industries, Inc.: www.rangerink.com

River City Rubberworks: www.rivercityrubberworks.com

Rubbermoon Stamp Company: www.rubbermoon.com

Rusty Pickle: www.rustypickle.com

Sanford: www.sanfordcorp.com

Scenic Route Paper Company: www.scenicroutepaper.com

Scrap Ease: http://scrapease.com

SEI: www.shopsei.com

Sharpie: www.sharpie.com

Small Studio Productions:
www.smallstudioproductions.com

Stampendous: www.stampendous.com

Stampers Anonymous: www.stampersanonymous.com

Stampin' Up!: www.stampinup.com

Stampington & Company: www.stampington.com

Stampotique Originals: www.stampotique.com

Stampscapes: www.stampscapes.com

Stewart Superior Corporation: www.stewartsuperior.com

Sugarloaf Products, Inc.: www.sugarloafproducts.com

Sunday International: www.sundayint.com

Suze Weinberg: www.schmoozewithsuze.com

Teemie's Blooms: www.teemiesblooms.com

Ten Seconds Studio: www.tensecondsstudio.com

Teters: www.teters.com

The Eggery Place: www.theeggeryplace.com

The Paper Company: www.paperco.co.uk/

The Queen's Dresser Drawers:
www.thequeensdresserdrawers.com

Therm O Web: www.thermoweb.com

Toybox Rubber Stamps: www.toyboxart.com

Triangle Crafts: Local Craft Store

Tsukineko: www.tsukineko.com

TweetyJill Publications: www.tweetyjill.com

USArtQuest, Inc.: www.usartquest.com

Velcro: www.velcro.com

Viva Las Vegastamps: www.vivalasvegastamps.com

Volcano Arts: www.volcanoartsbiz.com

Walnut Hollow: www.walnuthollow.com

Westwater Enterprises: Local Craft Store

Winsor & Newton: www.winsornewton.com

Zinsser: www.zinsser.com